The New Progressivism

The New Progressivism

A Grassroots Alternative to the Populism of
Our Times

David Amiel

Ismaël Emelien

Translated by Andrew Brown

polity

Originally published in French as *Le progrès ne tombe pas du ciel* © Librairie Arthème Fayard, 2019
This edition © Polity Press, 2020

Polity Press
65 Bridge Street
Cambridge CB2 1UR, UK

Polity Press
101 Station Landing
Suite 300
Medford, MA 02155, USA

ISBN-13: 978-1-5095-4141-6 (hardback)
ISBN-13: 978-1-5095-4142-3 (paperback)

A catalogue record for this book is available from the British Library.

Library of Congress Cataloging-in-Publication Data
Names: Amiel, David, author. | Emelien, Ismaël, author.
Title: The new progressivism : a grassroots alternative to the populism of out times / David Amiel, Ismaël Emelien ; translated by Andrew Brown.
Other titles: Progrès ne tombe pas du ciel. English
Description: Cambridge, UK ; Medford, MA : Polity, 2020. | Includes bibliographical references. | Summary: "The architects of Macron's success lay down the foundations for a new progressivism to counter the populism of our times"-- Provided by publisher.
Identifiers: LCCN 2019050900 (print) | LCCN 2019050901 (ebook) | ISBN 9781509541416 (hardback) | ISBN 9781509541423 (paperback) | ISBN 9781509541430 (epub)
Subjects: LCSH: Liberalism. | Populism. | Political participation--Social aspects. | Democracy. | Pluralism.
Classification: LCC JC574 .A43813 2020 (print) | LCC JC574 (ebook) | DDC 320.51/3--dc23
LC record available at https://lccn.loc.gov/2019050900
LC ebook record available at https://lccn.loc.gov/2019050901

Typeset in 12 on 15 pt Fournier MT by
Servis Filmsetting Ltd, Stockport, Cheshire
Printed and bound in Great Britain by CPI Group (UK) Ltd, Croyden

For further information on Polity, visit our website: politybooks.com

No man is an Iland, intire of itselfe; every man is a peece of the Continent, a part of the maine; if a Clod bee washed away by the Sea, Europe is the lesse, as well as if a Promontorie were, as well as if a Manor of thy friends or of thine owne were; any mans death diminishes me, because I am involved in Mankinde; And therefore never send to know for whom the bell tolls; It tolls for thee.

John Donne, *Devotions upon Emergent Occasions*, 1624

Contents

Acknowledgements

Thank you for reading this book! Do not hesitate to tell us what you thought about it: leprogresnetombepasduciel@protonmail.com

Thank you to the President of the Republic, Emmanuel Macron, for showing us that politics was a matter of conviction and that a benevolent determination could move mountains. Thank you also for placing in us the confidence of which we hope to be worthy every day.

Thanks to Alexis Kohler for showing us what total commitment in the service of the general interest means. Thank you also for listening patiently to our pleas, even at late hours of the day – absurdly late sometimes.

Thanks to Hanane and Eve, for their proofreading but also for their support, their presence – quite simply, their love.

Thank you to our parents, for (almost) everything.

Thanks to Sophie, our editor and (in spite of that) friend. Thanks to John, who saw it useful to have us translated – and to Andrew, who carried that exhausting task to the end. Thanks to all those who have read one or more of the many successive versions of this book, and whose benevolence has been equalled only by their rigour: Marcel, Thierry, Marie, Hubert, Timothée,

Acknowledgements

Léonore, Luc, Martin, Julien, François S., François T., Simon, Rémi, Ariane, Antoine A., Laurent, Dominique, Sylvain, Shahin, Jean-Francois, Antoine F., Daniel, Quentin.

Thanks to those who ensured that the past decade spent fighting for the ideas contained in this book was, first and foremost, a story of friendship, especially Stanislas, Cédric, Benjamin, Emmanuel, Julien, Sibeth, Quentin, Stéphane, Ludovic, Jean-Marie, Sylvain, Adrien, Nathalie, Alexander, Clément, Philippe.

Thank you to all the campaigners who have already shown that these ideas are worthwhile only if they are implemented, in particular (but not only!) Jean, Didier, Fanny, Clara, Missak, Juliette, Olivier, Thomas, Victor, Vincent, Thibault, Joé, Julien, Valérie, Christian, Grégoire P., Houda, Pacôme, Bensih, Bruno, Audrey, Aurélie, Mathieu, Zineb, Pauline, Marion, Grégoire D., Arnaud, Fatima, Serge, Selen, Mathieu, Marine M., Étienne, Paul-Hugo, Raphaël, Aziz-François, Marielle, Pénélope, Sandra, Marine B., Etienne, Stéphane, Aigline, Mathilde, Tess, Julie, Maëlle, Alexis, Jean, Christophe, Grégoire A., Pierre, Renaud, Léo, Caterina, Guillaume, Déborah, Éléonore, Schoitchi, Caroline, Frédéric, Philippe. Thank you to all those who enabled this legacy to prosper, at the headquarters of La République en Marche! and in all the territories of France. Our apologies to those who will not find their names here – this would have required several dozen more pages!

Introduction

In 2017, Emmanuel Macron was elected President of the French Republic. We were among those who helped to plan his En Marche! movement; we were responsible for the campaign strategy and its programme, and thus we both played a very active part in a political venture that most people viewed as impossible, namely the election of a man who had never run for office and who, a year earlier, had no party, no elected officials, no activists, and no funding. In a country marked by record levels of mistrust, we worked for the election of a man who proclaimed his confidence in the ability of ordinary citizens to return to the path of economic, social and political progress. In a country that had voted 'no' in the referendum on the European Constitutional Treaty in 2005, we worked for the election of a man who wore his commitment to the European project on his sleeve. In a country falling prey to populists who, both on the far left and the far right, shared a hatred of elites, we worked for the election of a man who had experience both as a banker and as a senior civil servant.

This election demonstrated one thing: the dice can always be rolled again. This is lucky, since the populists seem to have the wind in their sails worldwide: both in the old democracies

(France, Italy, Germany, the United States, the United Kingdom, Austria, Sweden, and others) and in 'illiberal democracies' (Hungary, Turkey, perhaps now Brazil?) and authoritarian countries (China, Russia, and most of their allies). So, is Emmanuel Macron's election an accident of history, a statistical blip together with the election of Donald Trump to the White House, Brexit, the triumph of the Five Star Movement and the Northern League in Italy, and the election of Jair Bolsonaro in Brazil? Or is it nothing but a French particularity? We do not think so.

To understand what is happening, it is less important to focus on these populist victories than on the defeats suffered by the old parties. The elections won by the populists are not enough to prove them right, but they undoubtedly demonstrate that the traditional political elites are wrong. They were wrong not to have spotted in time the flaws in the great narrative on which they had concurred since the fall of the Berlin Wall, namely the inexorable connection between democracy, liberalism and the market, in which popular support and economic development went hand in hand. The warning came from Asia, with the creation of a Chinese state, both capitalist and authoritarian; and the issue has also arisen in Eastern Europe, where it is claimed that 'democracy' is not the same as 'liberalism'. There is now a huge question mark hanging over the heart of the Western world, with an American president who rejects free trade and despises pluralism. The elites were wrong not to have understood that the 'progress' that seemed obvious to them – technological innovation, the globalization of trade, the extension of individual rights, cultural diversity – in fact only benefited an ever smaller minority of the population. They were wrong not to have seen how vehemently they were being rejected just when they seemed to have triumphed. But they are also wrong, now that they are weakened, just to stand by and watch in stupor as their opponents rise to power. They may cross their fingers in the hope these opponents will run out steam, but they are failing to supply themselves with the intellectual and political means to prepare a real counteroffensive.

The difficulties felt by a growing number of ordinary women and men do not all stem from the same origins, but they all produce the same symptoms: the feeling of having no place in society, of losing control of one's life and one's freedom to choose. A huge frustration has been mounting, often in silence. It was initially confined to the most marginal fringes of the population. It then spread to the lower classes, especially the workers. It is now shared by the middle classes. It has accommodated itself to populism, but it can represent an opportunity as it opens up an historic space for new progressivists, even if they are latecomers.

The race is on, and the latter are running short of time. Emmanuel Macron cuts a lonely figure at the table of the UN Security Council, or that of the G20, while the populists have already begun to unite and create their 'International' – think of the links between the American alt-right (mainly comprising Trump's most radical supporters) and the European far right, or the links that have existed for a long time between populists in Russia and in Latin America.

These forces are starting to organize, and we are convinced that Macron's success will not suffice to beat them. This battle, in France and abroad, cannot be fought by one man, or by one government, or even within one country. It is a political imperative: there are many people worldwide who are experimenting with innovative responses to populism, but they feel isolated. It is also a strategic imperative: the cruel irony of history is that populism rears its head again just when the need to act together across borders has never been stronger. Without a union of progressivists, there is, for example, no hope of curbing global warming or controlling economic globalization.

It was in order to contribute fully to this fight, one that takes place at all levels of society and beyond the borders of France that, after two years spent working as advisors to President Macron, we decided to leave.

Our first priority is to clarify some aims and methods of the new progressivism: this is the goal of the present book, which we wrote in the light of our French experience. For progressivists are no longer entitled, in any country, to make mistakes. We seek to win power, of course – and we here set out some potentially key elements for achieving this. But we also seek to exercise power – something often more difficult for progressivists than for populists.

This seems counter-intuitive. Many believe that electoral victory cannot be won without falling back on the tricks used by the populists: the lie (euphemized as 'alternative truth'); demagogy; and a virulent nationalism, often tinged with racism. In short, there is a widespread feeling that progressivists cannot win elections unless they ape their opponents. In 2017, Macron demonstrated that this was false: you can win by telling *the truth*, by avoiding engaging in personal attacks, trusting the intelligence of voters – and even by showing goodwill! You can win, above all, if you put forward a positive, exciting programme, one which touches the citizens' heartfelt expectations and is not limited to denouncing the madness of populists, or opportunistically welding together mere fragments of the electorate.

The same people assume that, once power has been won, the advantage will now lie with the progressivists, who will be able to draw on their skill, if not their experience, to run public affairs – while populists are often short of such skill and experience. Everyone can still remember how long the Trump administration needed to set itself up, or the game of musical chairs that ministers in the Brazilian populist Bolsonaro's government indulged in just weeks after it took office. Again, these people are wrong. Implementing progressivism is a daunting task. Progressivism is not a conservatism and, if it is to transform society, it needs to overcome all the forces of inertia ranged against it – particular interests, of course, but also, quite simply, habits. It must break with the politics of the old school, and in doing so it runs the risk of attracting the wrath of all the old guard, who hate the fact that the game is no longer played by the rules they had learned by heart and that they thought were immutable. But progressivism cannot resort to the simple slogans of populism, since society is not changed for the better by angry tweets or capricious decisions.

Progressivism needs to bring on board the majority in each country if it is to embark on its long adventure. To this end, it needs to make a proper diagnosis of society. It needs to say what it is itself, where it is going, for whom it is fighting; it needs to invent its own method. It needs to live up to people's expectations, and not to set out a hazy mixture of pragmatism, modernism and technical management: this has been, in too many countries, its natural temptation, one which distorts and weakens it. This is what, in France, Macron is taking great care to avoid. But it also needs to respond to the suspicions that it may arouse. What is its goal? Why (and for whom?) is it acting in this or that way? Today, its opponents are all too happy to answer on its behalf: they say it that it is acting for 'the rich', 'city dwellers' or 'the beneficiaries of globalization'.

We therefore wish, in these pages, to clarify a certain number of questions. We believe that progressivism is only beginning to spread across society; it is very far from having delivered its full potential. The most important thing, in our view, is not that we won an election or finally managed to hold the traditional political forces to account. The most important thing, in France, is to fulfil the promise of this victory, and to provoke, enliven, and strengthen progressivists everywhere else so that they in turn can tackle today's problems with the values and principles that we defend and – why not? – with the method we are proposing.

The purpose of this book is to bring together the new progressivists wherever they may live, beginning with those who are not even aware of each other's presence, and to provide them with a manifesto that will allow them to recognize each other and find guidance in current or future political debates. If we cite many concrete examples, this is simply to illustrate the principles that we are proposing, and to try to convince you of their scope.

We do not pretend to be academics. We do not pretend to have a ready-made programme, even less a full definition of the new progressivism. We do not wish to close the debate here but, on the contrary, to keep it open, and invite you to continue it. Based on our experience, we have no other ambition than to point out causes and ideas worth fighting for, and indicate a method to adopt. This book is binding only on us. But our secret hope is that it will encourage you too to play a part in politics, now that it has again become a great struggle.

I

The society of frustration

Imagine there's no heaven/It's easy if you try/No hell below us/
Above us only sky/Imagine all the people/Living for today …

John Lennon, 'Imagine', 1971

The opposition between left and right structured the political
life of the majority of Western countries for most of the twentieth century. However, the traditional parties that embodied
this situation are now marginalized (as in France and Italy),
running out of steam (as in Germany and Spain), severely
challenged (as in the United Kingdom) or deeply traumatized
(as in the United States, where Donald Trump has profoundly
shaken up the Republican Party). The phenomenon is so widespread that the simultaneity of these developments cannot be a
mere coincidence; rather, it represents the acceleration in recent
years of a phenomenon that has been ever more evident since
the 1970s, namely the exhaustion of a certain political system.
To understand it, we first need a brief historical retrospective.

The strange split between left and right

The triumph of the ideal of individual autonomy has been an essential factor of Western political life for the last two centuries.[1] For millennia, daily life consisted in accepting and carrying out the duties imposed by society as best one could. Power was an impenetrable thing that crushed ordinary men and women with all the weight of tradition: people obeyed their king, their lord, their paterfamilias; customs were followed, and it seemed unthinkable that a future could be both desirable and radically different from the past. With the Enlightenment, and the American and French revolutions, all this fell to pieces. The ideal, first fostered by the bourgeoisie, was now autonomy: people were to choose their own laws by the light of reason. In other words, the aim was to allow everyone to be in charge of their individual lives as far as possible, while participating as citizens in collective decision-making.

In theory, the individual no longer has to conform to society: it is up to society to organize itself around the individual. If some people wish to govern, they must do so for the happiness of the greatest number, and submit to their criticism as well as to their deliberations. That is what is called democracy: a community of free people governing themselves freely. Traditions no longer have any intrinsic value: we select from the past what suits us, and we invent what is lacking. That is what is called progress. In a word, the individual once had duties; now he or she mainly has rights.

This aspiration is not at all self-evident. Two centuries have been necessary for it to transform representations and realities. It was a radical innovation that first aroused two opposite reactions.[2]

One reaction consisted in saying that we must pursue this breakthrough in individual freedoms to its logical conclusion. We will call these people, for the sake of convenience, 'liberals', in a sense both broader than that which often prevails in the contemporary debate, and also broader than that which prevailed in the past. We include in this category both the British Liberal Party and many French Republicans of the late nineteenth century. This single term designates a political camp with many different incarnations and names, all of which shared one and the same fundamental aspiration. In the eyes of its followers, the need was to break all the chains that still hampered individuals, restricting their autonomy and preventing them from expressing their singularity. Against tradition, the 'liberals' defended the right to divorce, for example. Against arbitrary power, they defended the right to vote, freedom of expression and the right to a fair trial. Against corporations, they defended the right to conduct business as one wishes, and to enter into contracts freely.

Another reaction, however, cast a more critical eye on the claim of empowering individuals. These critics were themselves divided into two antagonistic trends. There were the conservatives, who defended all the Bastilles that liberalism aimed to bring down: they defended the monarchy against the republic, the Church against free thought, the patriarchal model of the family against the emancipation of women and new customs, and so on. Then there were the Marxists, who also contested, albeit in a radically different way, the autonomy of the individual as 'liberals' presented it.[3] They considered that 'workers' did indeed have the right to vote, but were in fact subject to capitalist exploitation, and had no say in choosing their daily destiny. To achieve true autonomy, true freedom, they had first to recognize themselves as members of a social class (the proletariat), organize themselves into a party, prepare for revolution, seize power, and only then, after having gained experience under the dictatorship of the proletariat, would they be able to live fully as autonomous individuals. Thus, conservatives and Marxists refused to countenance establishing autonomy for individuals even if this refusal was definitive for the former and only temporary for the latter.

This tableau, distinguishing between conservatives, Marxists and 'liberals', is a schematic and deliberately simplistic way of representing the great currents that dominated the debate in most European countries at the end of the nineteenth century.

The twentieth century has changed the picture dramatically. The categories persist in a more or less underground fashion (there are still Marxists, conservatives, and 'liberals') but the most significant split, the one that forges electoral alliances, allows people to place themselves politically in a certain camp, and drives debates in Parliament as well as at family meals, became the split between left and right. It spread far beyond Europe to most democracies. This split has older roots, but it has also played a major and familiar role until quite recently.[4]

At first sight, however, this split is an oddity: after all, each camp was divided within itself – on the left, between left-wing 'liberals' and Marxists, and on the right, between right-wing 'liberals' and conservatives.

For 'left-wing liberals', often active in social democratic, democratic or socialist parties, the economic priority is equality. In their view, the order created spontaneously by capitalism and the market economy is neither necessarily fair nor always efficient. For example, the fact that workers cannot provide themselves with medical care, and that children cannot educate themselves naturally, limits the autonomy of the individual. Thus, 'left-wing liberals' help to set up mechanisms of redistribution and protection, including progressive taxation, free public services and national insurance. Moreover, in social matters, they remain the foremost defenders of the extension of individual rights and public freedoms. For 'right-wing liberals', on the other hand, in economic matters, the priority is freedom – the freedom to be an entrepreneur, to create, to innovate and to trade. However, they are afraid of anything that might threaten the economic order, and there are many occasions where they are the allies of the conservatives and willingly share the reluctance of the latter to change society. Throughout their history, they have been quite prepared to adopt repressive positions on matters of security, and traditionalist positions vis-à-vis morals, the family and religion.

This helps to explain the raison d'être of the split between 'right' and 'left'.

In their different camps, 'liberals' tempered the extremes and gradually contributed to their normalization. Little by little, most parties of the left as well as of the right converged on a regulated market economy, combining the dynamism of capitalism with the stability offered by the welfare state, simultaneously improving both the fairness and the efficiency of our economies. Little by little, most conservatives resigned themselves to social change and defended ever narrower stances (as with their opposition to women's right to vote, to abortion, to same-sex marriage, and to assisted reproductive technology).

'Left-wing liberals' and 'right-wing liberals' in turn helped to create a desirable order. 'Left-wing liberals' – often working via social democratic or socialist parties – provided the necessary redistribution of wealth and social progress. 'Right-wing liberals' provided the necessary economic energy and, by acting as guides for the conservative neighbours with whom they often coexisted in the same political formations, they also made it possible to adapt cultural change to the public's mindset.

The ideal of autonomy seems to have hardly any substantial ideological alternatives in the West. This triumph is evident both at the political and social levels. The last monumental ideological rival, communism, collapsed in the second half of the twentieth century. As we shall see, even Western populism (that of Trump, Le Pen, Salvini, etc.) feeds on this democratic rhetoric, even if it wishes to pervert the institutions that actually make such rhetoric possible. When we look at ordinary citizens, it is spectacular how the idea that everyone should be allowed to improve his social position (as opposed to the conservative emphasis on inheritance) but through individual efforts (as opposed to the socialist 'class struggles') has triumphed. It is especially striking, for instance, to see that working-class employees simply aspire to see their efforts rewarded and therefore can be as quick to denounce the 'profiteers' above them as those existing 'on welfare' below (an idea that populism has been particularly good at exploiting). The problem is that their efforts are not rewarded.

The promise betrayed

Let's get back to the current situation. It is far from being the 'best of all worlds' for which the preceding fresco might have led us to hope. A wave of revolt is blowing through the wealthy nations of Europe and America as well as the poorer nations such as Brazil, in multicultural societies, such as the United Kingdom, and more homogenous societies, such as Italy, in countries where inequalities in income have risen dramatically, such as the United States, and in countries that have contained these inequalities thanks to a high level of redistribution, such as France.

In each case, however, this revolt expresses the same frustration. We can understand it only if we examine citizens' expectations – that is to say, in the final analysis, the implicit promise that society made to them, a promise that has obviously not been met. What was this promise? The greatest level of autonomy for all, in other words the ability of individuals to control as far as possible the essential parameters of their lives.

In the case of Western countries, the golden age of this ideal was reached between the 1960s and the 1980s. It is hardly surprising if this was also the period in which alternatives to liberal democracy ran out of steam. All the signs seemed to promise that individuals would now have the means to attain their ambitions: economic growth and mass education, progress in individual rights and the collapse of religious and patriarchal authority, the independence and democratization of the developing countries and the defeat of totalitarianism. It had never been so easy to believe that you could define your existence by your work, your efforts, your merits – by moving elsewhere, if necessary, to pursue your dreams, or by climbing the social ladder to forge your own destiny.

The hour of a new humanism seemed to have struck. But it never struck for everyone. Over the next forty years, the promise that had been drummed into everyone's head began to seem increasingly hollow. The gap has grown between words and realities and has now reached a breaking point.

We are enjoined (in the media, in businesses, at school) to seize new 'opportunities'. Yet this ubiquitous call in fact speaks only to a few. The daily life of the vast majority is made up of diminishing possibilities and multiple segregations, both insidious and manifest. Despite the promise of 'moving forward' made to everyone, the reality is that most of us are going through a time of great immobility.[5] We are victims of an optical illusion, as when you're under the impression that the train you've boarded is moving forward, while in fact it's still at the platform – it's the other trains that you can see through the window that are moving.

True, over the last forty years there have been many changes.

We do not underestimate them. Family models have evolved, jobs and career paths too, as well as lifestyles. But the initial promise was that the sum of these changes would produce individual and collective progress and allow people to choose their lives more freely. The reality is different: these changes gave rise to great hopes in people's minds, but lead to considerable disappointment in their real lives. What we are told is contradicted by the realities we experience.

The social message to women is that, for the first time in millennia, they are free to find fulfilment – but the reality is that they are still paid less than men, even in those nations that think they have conquered these prejudices (women earn 16 per cent less in the European Union, and more than 20 per cent less in Germany and the United Kingdom).[6] Women continue to perform the vast majority of household chores; having children slows down their professional advancement; and not until #MeToo did modern societies re-examine the ways in which they continued to tolerate the mistreatment of their women, despite decades of progress in the female condition.

Similarly, the social message to legal immigrants is that they just need to work hard at school and respect the law, and then they will have the same opportunities as everyone else. The reality is that they are still hugely discriminated against. For example, in the United States, given equal skills and experience, job applicants whose names indicate that the colour of their skin is 'white' are contacted 50 per cent more frequently after submitting a CV as those whose name indicates that their skin is 'black'. The researchers who conducted this study[7] calculated that having a 'white' name was equivalent to having eight more years' experience compared to the CV of a person with a 'black' name who was just as highly qualified. Worse, a French study recently revealed that sometimes the higher your level of education, the higher the discrimination you can face in the jobs market. A French person, for example, with a name perceived as Muslim is more discriminated against if he has five years of higher education than if he has just two.[8]

In the same way, the message addressed to the employees of the most innovative companies is hypocritical: the dominant managerial culture calls on everyone to 'take the initiative', 'be dynamic' and 'innovate'. But in reality, daily pressure is intensifying and the minute scrutiny of employees is increasing:[9] it is no coincidence that Amazon is both one of the most robotized companies in the world and the place where a new sense of alienation from work is regularly expressed. It is easy to understand why a growing number of employees now feel 'surplus to requirements', 'useless', or feel that they are doing 'bullshit jobs'.

The promises and the realities seem to have gone their separate ways. At the same time, YouTube and Netflix offer virtually every inhabitant of the planet a window on the reality of the tiny minority for whom the promise of autonomy has been fulfilled. That is why we all live in a society of frustration. What distinguishes between us is less and less what we aspire to: it is what we actually have.

Social, geographical and economic immobility

Frustration mainly stems from social immobility. We are told about 'meritocracy', suggesting that if there are inequalities in our society, they are essentially fair inequalities, since everyone can escape from them by dint of effort, work, and personal talent. The problem is not with the concept, as many too hastily claim, but with the reality: there are innumerable illegitimate and often insurmountable barriers that face people born in the working class. Worse, in many countries things are deteriorating. Injustice often begins at kindergarten level, with highly unequal access to education and health. This is because, if there are few second chances, in actual fact there are no first chances either: statistically, it takes more than five generations in the United States and Italy, six in Germany and Hungary, and nine in Brazil and South Africa for a family that is today among the poorest ten per cent to climb the ladder up into the middle class.[10] What about France, the 'land of equality'? More than six generations even here! And injustice is no longer remedied over the course of one's overall career, due to the transformations of the economy that have not been supplemented by improving continuing education. In the past, a skilled automobile worker could hope to rise, by merit and promotion, to the status of executive. How could he possibly do so today, when he works for the subcontractor of a big brand, and when workers and managers are no longer part of the same company?[11]

Aside from economics, we are often told about the 'social mix', informed that professions matter less than they used to, that cultural homogeneity has grown and social prejudices have been reduced, that personality counts more than milieu and that we are now able to socialize with any of our fellow citizens. However, this so-called 'social mix' is everywhere on the retreat. In France, for example, the paths of rich and poor used to cross in the same apartment buildings,[12] with the former occupying the ground floor and the latter living on the upper storeys. Until more recently, they would still encounter each other in the same neighbourhood. Nowadays, they do not even see each other any more: according to economist Éric Maurin, half of the French are not acquainted with any employee in their neighbourhood who earns more than 3,500 euros net per month (that is, who belongs to the wealthiest ten per cent).[13] This is true even in private life. We marry those who are like us. A man with a master's degree is seven times more likely to have a partner of the same kind than one without a degree.[14]

Secondly, frustration comes from geographical immobility. Every day we hear of 'metropolises' where, it seems, life is good: New York or Berlin, Paris or London – this is where we would need to live if we wanted to make our fortune. And it's true: this is where the best universities, the best jobs, the best public services and the most promising neighbourhoods are concentrated. The reasons are obvious. Traditional industries needed raw materials: in the United States they developed in the Appalachians, in the United Kingdom in Yorkshire, in France in the North – in short, wherever coal was found. The raw material needed by the cutting-edge sectors (new technology, finance, communication, etc.) is diversified talents, and infrastructures linking them with the rest of the world: these days, they therefore develop in the big cities, as this is where the most highly educated populations and the most efficient airports are found. This split is becoming more visible every day.

So, experts, ministry spokespersons and journalists soon start telling desperate workers, and more generally all who are finding it difficult to get a job, to be mobile, to leave home, to migrate to the big cities. Yet when we look at the statistics, mobility is not increasing. Why? Because big cities have become impregnable fortresses. Who can move to them nowadays? Space is limited, and it's impossible – or almost impossible – to put up new buildings in them. Competition for an apartment is fierce. In New York, real estate today is 30 per cent more expensive than ten years ago.[15] In the biggest German cities, real estate prices rose by an average of 80 per cent between 2009 and 2017.[16] In London, the increase since 2010 has been around 50 per cent.[17] To rent an apartment in these cities, you need a guarantor with a comfortable income – unless you yourself have a particularly high salary. It has become almost impossible to buy unless you have wealthy parents: according to Thomas Piketty's calculations, '[I]nherited wealth once again accounted for the majority of wealth in the 1980s, and according to the latest available figures it represents roughly two-thirds of private capital in France in 2010, compared with barely one-third of capital accumulated from savings'.[18] This problem seems to exist right across Europe. In Germany, which started from a more egalitarian situation, the annual flow of succession has increased five-fold since the 1960s, and it has also risen significantly in the United Kingdom.[19] Everything suggests that things will get worse. Increasingly, privileged families will pass on to their members the right to live in those places where wealth is created. Increasingly, the rest will be pushed back to the outskirts of the metropolises, even further away than the suburbs, kept at a distance by this new class of rentiers. This is serious, because housing is not an ordinary good – it is the good that opens the way to other goods: training, social relations, a profession. The problem is not that there is such a thing as heirs – handing down one's property is perfectly natural. The problem is that if we continue passively to observe these territorial transformations, we will no longer be able to do anything unless we are likely to inherit a significant amount of wealth.

Finally, frustration stems from economic immobility. We are presented with a new economic world, full of opportunities to move from one company to another, to practise several trades in our lives, to build up unique careers by expanding, step by step, our skill set. But, in fact it is clear that career diversification has mainly been a fig-leaf for career insecurity: the youngest are condemned, in the name of a marketing discourse that extols their 'freedom', to wander from internships to precarious contracts. On the one hand, the revolutions in digital technology, artificial intelligence and biotechnology are constantly being vaunted: there are new professions in these areas, or so we are told, new opportunities that we should all seize. On the other hand, we are forced to the conclusion that economic growth is stalling. On the one hand, we are told of an economy of 'disruption', where no job is ever definitively safe, and on the other hand, we can see that the average age of companies is constantly rising – in any case in the United States and in many European countries.[20]

So, the right question is: why doesn't technology help us make our jobs more fulfilling, more rewarding, more remunerative? Where has innovation gone? The answer is simple: it has been confiscated by just a few people – or, more specifically, by just a few companies. The gap between them and the rest of the economy has widened considerably. In the past, innovation spread out gradually from the main companies to the rest of the economy; now, it is, so to speak, monopolized by the former.

People will retort that we must be patient: months or even years are needed to train today's employees to work in the new sectors. However, it's not just a matter of time: the obstacles that hold back innovation are often far from natural. First of all, of course, there are the professions that feel threatened by technology, and therefore do everything to delay its deployment: the confrontation between taxi drivers, who have been benefiting for decades from expensive licences, and drivers registered on platforms (Blacklane, Gett, Uber, etc.), who are more available and can charge lower prices, has long been emblematic of this. There is no doubt, however, that the transition from one model to another was desirable: the gradual expansion of platforms made it possible to offer many jobs to low-skilled jobless people, though it has been insufficiently supplemented by new social rights.

But there are also all the big innovative companies that want to keep technology to themselves, for their own exclusive benefit, by doing all in their power to prevent the emergence of competitors. We do not realize this, because these battles are less visible: they are conducted in the seclusion of research and development laboratories, sometimes in law firms, rarely in public. Nobel-prize winning economist Joseph E. Stiglitz is probably one of the most famous intellectuals to have underlined how 'rent-seeking' of the sort has become a defining feature of American economic life at the expense of workers, consumers and growth. He gives the example of the American firm Myriad that patented the identification of certain genes related to breast cancer: it extracted excessive profits from tests designed to detect a risk of this cancer, to the detriment of patients and while preventing other researchers and doctors from building on this discovery until the US Supreme Court intervened in 2013.[21] Other companies may rely on the very structure of the market and the characteristics of the goods they produce. In this respect, one of the most spectacular ways in which competition has diminished is found within the very sector that should be the most dynamic, namely IT. Here, the winner does not take the biggest share of the cake: the winner spontaneously takes *all* the cake. This is partly due to the nature of the services offered. A company wants to be referenced on Google because this is the search engine that consumers use. And consumers use Google because it is on this search engine that companies are most clearly referenced. Once all businesses and consumers use Google, it becomes almost impossible to launch a new search engine. Google has more than a 90 per cent share of the global market. We could follow the same reasoning with regard to Facebook. A company could create a new and better-constructed social network, one that is more aesthetic and more user-friendly, and in particular more respectful of privacy. But people will stay on Facebook simply because other people are on Facebook. So it is that the digital giants believe their thrones are secure.

These situations illustrate a more general risk: the march towards monopoly. This can be detected in many other areas. Entire sectors of our economy have managed to shelter from competitors who might offer cheaper or better supplies, thus creating jobs and purchasing power. Even in the United States, which is the supposed vanguard of competition, the concentration of the economy has grown steadily.

The invisible culprit

These immobilities radically undermine our society. This is a loss, of course, for all those who are condemned to stagnate: their desire for betterment comes up against a glass ceiling. But it is also a loss for the community as a whole. Talents that are useful to everyone – economic, social, artistic – remain fallow. Fruitful encounters do not take place. Friction is needed to strike a spark. The impact can be found well beyond the realm of socio-economic dynamics to which we have referred so far.

There is no better example of this than culture. In 1961, Robert Allen Zimmerman, who was born and raised in Minnesota, settled in Greenwich Village, New York, without a penny in his pocket. In this melting-pot, he met folk singers as well as students at Columbia University, bluesmen as well as lovers of literature. He developed a unique style based on musical and literary experiment. Today, he would never be able to afford to live in Manhattan; he would just have continued playing guitar in Minnesota. Without these meetings, would Robert Allen Zimmerman have become Bob Dylan? The effect of social immobility on the cultural world cannot be overemphasized. Our films today are too often franchises dragged out into endless episodes – from *X-Men* to *Star Wars*. Our fashions are all too often 'retro' or 'vintage'. Our music is too often a remix. Our stars are too often the children of aging stars. It has not always been this way.

In short, our society is a society of frustration. We do not suffer from too much innovation, but from too little. We do not suffer from too much mobility, but too little. We all live more and more curled up in our bastions, observing the world through a narrow window.

We progressivists are much more pragmatic than the populists: we do not think it is desirable to change from one society to another; and we are much more idealistic than the conservatives, because we believe that it is possible and even necessary to change society as such.

The gap between the promise of individual autonomy and the shrinking of our lives has created a colossal disappointment. So colossal that it becomes incomprehensible. We then look for a culprit. Paradoxically, the most immediate reaction is to think that we are ourselves the culprit. We are trained to believe that our fate is in our own hands: if we fail, who else do we have to blame but ourselves? The first essential step is to understand that it is not usually an individual problem, but a collective problem. The vast majority of individuals have legitimate reasons to consider themselves frustrated and unfairly treated. There is reason enough to revolt. But the question is: to revolt against *what*, exactly? In politics, it is easy to designate an enemy and to stage a battle. Today there are too many options to choose between: the 'one per cent' against the '99 per cent', the people against the oligarchy, the foreigner against the native, the metropolises against the peripheries, etc.

In our turn, we could ask for heads to roll – it's easy to channel resentments by pointing the finger at someone to pillory. But if it were that simple, countries where populist leaders have come to power ought gradually to have become more tranquil and stable as their programme was implemented. It's quite the opposite. Failing to identify the ills of the country, these populists are forced to launch a permanent denunciation of new enemies – the press, central banks, immigrants, supra-national institutions such as the EU – so as to hide their own inability to deal with the complexities of reality.

Of course, those with the best standard of living in our society must certainly accept the loss of some of their privileges when this is the price to be paid to open up these privileges to all; we will come back to this. But it is useless to theatricalize the confrontation, since it is not a goal in itself. The progressivist has an opponent. But our opponent is not *someone*, but *something*. It's not the rentier, but monopoly.

Political monopolies

The first opponent of the progressivist is political monopoly: all too often it has led to a fossilization of democratic life. It is striking to see how, in most of the world's major democracies, and sometimes dating back to the establishment of the relevant democracy or republic itself, political power has been monopolized by an old oligopoly consisting of only two or three players: Democrats and Republicans in the United States, Labour and Conservatives in the United Kingdom, the CDU and SPD in Germany, the PSOE and the People's Party in Spain, the PAN, PRD and PRI in Mexico, the PLD and PDJ in Japan, the ANC in South Africa, the Socialist Party and the RPR/UMP/LR in France – and this is only the beginning of a list that could be considerably longer!

In principle, there is nothing wrong with this. It is for the most part the fruit of a long history, one which triggers memories, loyalties and attachments, as we noted at the beginning of our chapter. But their responsibility for the wave of apathy and disengagement, to which they are everywhere falling victim, is immense. There are at least three reasons for this.

The first reason is the least cruel: they have in a way done their job. At the end of the twentieth century, after spectacular struggles, the governing parties had almost everywhere settled their great historical quarrel. Until then, the fight was for or against capitalism. Almost everywhere, the market economy has established itself, consecrating the freedom of economic initiative. Its constraints were gradually accepted by all major

European parties, and three particularly symbolic dates illustrate this process: 1959, when the German SPD bade farewell to Marxism; 1983, when the French socialists chose to make the French economy part of a European framework; and 1995, when the British Labour Party abandoned its commitment to mass nationalization. At the same time, social mechanisms have been put in place to help, at the very least, those who need it most. European Union member countries today enjoy an unprecedented degree of redistribution: on average, 40 per cent of the wealth they produce goes on taxes or insurance contributions. Yet, even when a right-wing party is in power, nobody suggests dismantling this system.

The fight was also for or against more rights, both political and individual. Almost everywhere, democracy has established itself as a manifest ideal, and considerable personal freedoms have been achieved. Same-sex marriage has been legalized simultaneously in many countries over the last ten years or so: despite changing governments, it has not been called into question since. Clearly, there are still lively debates on these large-scale social issues, but they seem secondary compared to those that occupied us in the past, and in any case they do not give rise to intense opposition or support, except in ever smaller sectors of the population.

On the other hand, the traditional parties have not been able to set themselves new objectives, and this is the second reason for their decline. However, there is no lack of topics of major importance for our individual and collective futures, wherever we may live: global warming and the disappearance of biodiversity, globalization, territorial divides and multiculturalism, not to mention transhumanism and artificial intelligence. On all these subjects, the political world lags drastically behind civil society. A century ago, political activists were in the vanguard of society, shouting, 'Follow us!' Today, it is the citizens who are asking political activists, 'But where exactly are you?' On none of these great issues have traditional parties been able to formulate a doctrine or to implement a policy likely to provide them with a real solution. Let's pick up some of those mentioned in the previous pages: they all fall into the black hole of political debate. The fight against monopolies is not supported by anyone: the left does not want to give the impression of giving succour to competition, the right does not want to be seen to put big business at a disadvantage. The same applies to geographical inequalities: the right ignores inequality, the left ignores geography.

This spectacular incapacity of the body politic to adapt to the expectations of the electorate stems, in the last resort, from one simple factor: lack of competition. For a long time, it seemed particularly difficult to create a new party ex nihilo. How do you get the voters to recognize you? How do you raise money? How do you mobilize activists? Everything follows on from this.

This is the reason why the traditional parties tolerated more and more divisions within themselves: it was better to be a big, disunited party than a united but small one. The need to control immigration more stringently, for example, has been as much a subject for debate on the left as on the right. The relationship to the EU is also a subject that divides people within European political groupings just as much as it cuts between these different groupings. One might have supposed that a realignment was taking place, given the widening disagreements that necessitate new structures of political expression. This has sometimes been tried, but without success, as with Die Linke in Germany. It was too risky for candidates for election to stray from the beaten path: it was better to make do with a divided but recognizable party. The result is that the left and the right now agree on too many things for their regular power swaps to create any real alternatives: voters increasingly feel that, once the election campaign is over, the policies pursued will be somewhat identical whoever wins. Yet left and right are unable to move forward together: no constructive coalition is possible when everyone is forced to compromise with the most extreme tendencies in his or her camp. So, we have been condemned to have neither productive handovers of power, nor new majorities: an oligopoly of impotence.

The regular exercise of power has also created its own difficulties. By becoming state managers, our rulers have tended to reduce politics to a series of technical problems that can be solved by government policies. Political programmes have become more and more precise, to the detriment of the bigger picture, more and more alike, to the detriment of the desire for transformation, and more and more economic and technical, to the detriment of all the other dimensions of political life. Far from politics being able to control and guide the great transformations we are talking about, it has been reduced to a series of technical adjustments in various ministerial departments. The professionalization that accompanied positions of responsibility came with an increasing apathy on the part of grassroots activists: the close link with ordinary people's concerns broke down, and politicians gradually envisaged society first and foremost through media spin and opinion polls that were often an inadequate reflection of reality. Thus, when En Marche! launched its first door-to-door operation in July 2016, its members were surprised by the huge number of women from all walks of life who described the sexual harassment they faced; this led Emmanuel Macron, who was then running for president, to promise to make this the main cause of his five-year term. Traditional observers jeered ... until #MeToo hit the headlines a year later.

Lack of interest among voters was demonstrated both by their increasing disillusionment and often by their simply staying at home when elections were called. But this frustration found few outlets. The most profitable way to maintain power has long consisted not in trying to win back disappointed voters, but in cultivating your base: in a shrinking cake, you had to try to keep the biggest share. The bulk of a party's energy has gradually become devoted firstly to mobilizing its supporters when in opposition (even by making untenable promises, or attacking government policies for the simple reason that the opposition was not responsible for them), and secondly to retaining the loyalty of a few fractions of the electorate once in power. Parties gave up having any overall plan: they saw this as neither necessary in principle nor as having any electoral advantage. The American Democrats concentrated their efforts on the large population of the Atlantic and Pacific coasts, and thought they could give up on the middle classes of the Midwest, which were supposed to be irretrievably Republican. The British Labour Party concentrated on the employees of large companies and the residents of large cities, neglecting to speak to the working classes who were bearing the brunt of globalization. When different parties come to power, they no longer represent any real alternatives. Yesterday, political parties each represented a specific camp, a part of society. Today, they are widely seen as defending the same camp – their own – and representing only themselves. They have moved from the defence of the public interest to the pursuit of their own electoral interest.

This situation has become untenable. The social frustration that has resulted is now out of control, while support for traditional parties has gradually declined. We have seen the emergence or rebirth, little by little, of new players: the Greens in Germany, the Rassemblement National in France, UKIP, the Brexit Party and the Lib-Dems in the United Kingdom, etc. Things are now accelerating. The advantage once taken for granted by the political oligopoly is being questioned. New technologies make it possible to create movements much more quickly than in the past, whether these be social movements (Occupy Wall Street, Indignados, the yellow vests) or political movements (En Marche!, Ciudadanos, the Five Star Movement), and they now throw up atypical figures such as Donald Trump and Bernie Sanders. The political oligopoly is cracking on all sides. The time has come to re-examine the fundamental objectives that we wish to pursue.

2

Maximizing possibilities
(or the first principle of progressivism)

Every champion was once a contender
that refused to give up.

Sylvester Stallone, *Rocky Balboa*, 2006

What can we expect from politics? What progress can it bring?
We don't ask politics to give us happiness itself, once and for
all. We have learned, sometimes painfully, that no one has the
general recipe for this ('what makes *human beings* happy?'), let
alone the particular ingredients ('what would make *me* happy?').
We are therefore definitely condemned, at the individual and
collective level, to hesitation, to discussion, to trial and error.
On the other hand, we always expect politics to provide us with
the means to pursue a better future. What we want to be able to
do with these means is to deploy our talents and abilities so we
can 'pursue happiness', through reason, effort and deliberation,
both individually as persons, and at the collective level as citizens. This demanding project bears, as we have seen, the name
'autonomy'.

This is the progress that our progressivism seeks to foster.
It is a human progress. It is faithful to the founding ideals of
the eighteenth century but departs from the naive conceptions

with which the nineteenth century sullied the notion, making us wrongly believe that the irresistible deployment of science would spontaneously lead to a better society. It is obvious that we can no longer claim that humanity naturally rises in moral level as history advances. This hope was reduced to zero by the tragedies of the twentieth century, the century of Auschwitz and the Gulag. But we cannot even argue that technological progress is always beneficial: the environmental crisis reminds us of this every day. The human progress of which we speak can no longer be an irresistible march towards a better future. It is of a different essence, fragile and perishable, capable of advances but also of retreats. It cherishes inherited elements, be these the greatest achievements of the arts or the wonders of nature. It looks without contempt at the past, without certainty at the future, but without resignation at the present, whose challenges can be met.

To better meet the challenges autonomy needs to address, we have to examine how it manifests itself. We have seen that it has a double dimension, individual and collective. Firstly, what does autonomy mean at the individual level? We define it in a simple principle: 'maximizing the possibilities of individuals, both in the present and the future'.

'Maximizing the possibilities': this means that the progressivists' mission is to do everything in their power to expand the opportunities and horizons of individuals; to enable them to pursue their talents, their abilities; to help them engage in more promising or longer-term studies; to allow them to obtain a better reward for their efforts; to reward their commitment to others or their artistic creativity; to support scientific research, etc. It's not a luxury. It means protecting the freedom of everyone to control their lives as much as possible, at least as far as the main parameters are concerned: their professions, at a time of slowing economic and social mobility; their place of residence, at a time of geographical immobility provoked by the metropolitanization of societies; their beliefs, at a time of intensifying religious fundamentalism; their opinions, at a time when social networks are confining us within narrow circles of convictions, etc. This perspective is more controversial than it seems. It means, for example, that the problem stems more from injustice than from inequality, at a time when many observers are more interested in the latter than in the former. In our view, this is a central point. France, for example, has not experienced a significant increase in income inequality since General de Gaulle: the problem isn't that an executive always earns more than an employee, it's that an employee can no longer become an executive. Likewise, even in the United States (where it seems essential to reduce income inequality, which has grown so dramatically that the rules of the game are deeply biased in favour of a narrow elite), a mere bill to tax high incomes would not be enough, as it would not in itself restore the 'possibilities' of the American working classes.

Then come 'individuals': progressivists no longer address social classes, but people. Of course, you are first and foremost defined by your income, your parents' jobs and where you live. But the evolution of our societies and the digital revolution have theoretically brought us closer than ever before to the time when everyone will be considered as a true individual. This increasing individualization has been noted on numerous occasions in recent decades. It has been observed that the simple categories on which political activists thrived in the first half of the twentieth century (the category of the 'working class', in this case), since these categories effectively made it possible to decipher and predict people's behaviour and aspirations, have lost their relevance. Social determinants still weigh heavily, but they have become much more complex: the place where one lives, to take just one example, creates specific characteristics, and middle-class employees who manage to live in a big metropolis can provide their children with a very different future as compared with employees who have very similar incomes but live in a remote area where public services are dwindling, where education is deteriorating, and where companies are closing down one after the other. Above all, being treated first and foremost as individuals is what we aspire to subjectively: we want the legitimacy of our personal aspirations to be recognized, we want to be endowed with the means to overcome the specific obstacles to this process, we want to become free to choose our own lives ourselves. This is exactly what matters to us: everyone should be able to follow his or her own path. For this to be achieved, politics must shift from ready-to-wear to tailor-made solutions.

'In the present and the future', finally. What we do on any one day will obviously shape what happens to us the next day. A government must constantly seek a balance between the interests of present and future generations – this is where the question of public debt comes up. But what is new about the twenty-first century, as we face global warming, dwindling biodiversity and increasing pollution, is that the decisions governments are making today irreversibly determine the 'possibilities' of future generations. Above a certain level of greenhouse gas emissions, it will no longer be possible for our heirs to limit global warming. We are not talking about an additional cost for one or more future generations, like the repayment of excessive financial debt, for example. Far from it: we are talking about a permanent worsening of the living conditions of humanity as a whole.

Equality of opportunity is not an opportunity for equality

Some may think that 'maximizing the possibilities' is just another way of talking about 'equality of opportunity', a notion that political parties, left and right, Democrats and Republicans, Labour and Conservatives, have been using for many years now. This is, however, not the case.

What does 'equality of opportunity' mean? It means that one's origins should not impact on the choice of one's destiny. It is an essential criterion of both justice and efficiency, and one which we obviously endorse.

Should we use this expression to summarize our approach? We do not believe so: it is in fact an inadequate notion.

It is inadequate in terms of its duration: equality of opportunity is a static notion, one that consists in believing that equality at the beginning of life will ensure equality throughout life. On this view, it is enough to ensure, starting in childhood, that the competition is fair and that everyone sets off from the same starting line – the result doesn't matter. But this ignores the fact that, during the race, people stumble. Some have accidents and some do not. Some go through moments of weakness and doubt, while others enjoy beneficial encounters and strokes of luck. It is therefore at all times of life that we need to ensure that everyone can reach his or her full potential, and help those who have fallen to get back on their feet.

It is also inadequate in terms of its scope: equality of opportunity tells us nothing about environmental, ethical or cultural issues. In reality, it has nothing to say about anything except the mere competition for economic and social places. And even in the economic field, it cannot tell us whether it is better to have strong or weak growth, while in the social realm it cannot tell us what kind of education is needed, just as long as it is the same quality for all. It is therefore a means, and in no way an end. So it is impossible for progressivists to be satisfied with 'equality of opportunity' as the ultimate goal.

Let's move on to political strategy. Many continue to believe that 'equality of opportunity', if it is inadequate as an end, is still a very useful slogan, one that can mobilize citizens. Everything, however, points to the opposite. The more 'equality of opportunity' has been used by the parties of left and right, the more it has actually declined.

We can see this when it comes to inherited wealth. Nothing re-sets the counter to zero at the moment of birth better than the regulation of very large inheritances. This should logically be the priority for all those who fight for equality of opportunity. Is it not unfair, from the point of view of equality of opportunity, for a lazy person born into a very wealthy family to benefit from millions of euros that a hard worker from a modest family will never manage to accumulate? However, in France, the most unpopular tax is precisely inheritance tax – partly through ignorance of the rates actually applied, but also for other reasons (often because people hope to pass on a higher inheritance than they actually will, but sometimes because the principle of taxing the wealth accumulated over a whole lifetime at the time of death is deemed unfair). Any politician who would venture to make a proposal on the subject therefore automatically runs the risk of electoral disaster, whichever continent he or she may live on.

The same is true in the field of education. For equality of opportunity to progress, the cultural heritage needs to be better shared. Is it not unfair that poor children are statistically condemned, from the earliest age, to second-class fates simply because they have a smaller vocabulary than children of the same age from wealthy families – because their parents talk to them less, stimulate them less, and plonk then down in front of screens more often? Yet equality of opportunity is not to everyone's taste. Parents able to do so are not only willing to spend considerable sums of money to ensure that their children can attend the best schools, but also, when they succeed in this, they devote an equal amount of energy to ensuring that their offspring are not exposed to social diversity. Thus, from Toronto to Singapore, and from Pretoria to Paris, the slightest suggestion that children from the lower classes might gain access to schools previously reserved for the middle or upper classes triggers unusually fierce debates.

The result is clear: despite forty years of fighting for equality of opportunity, any such equality has actually declined. This is a fact that progressivists must take into account.

How are we to explain this incredible paradox? The answer is simple: the expression 'equality of opportunity' failed to rally enough support, as it became exclusively synonymous with a zero-sum game. Rightly or wrongly, it suggested that anything one gave to some people had to be taken from others. Rightly or wrongly, it gave the impression that everything was going to be uniformized from below. Rightly or wrongly, everyone felt threatened. As a result, equality of opportunity has often been unacceptable in practice, even though it is quite rightly attractive in theory.

To speak exclusively of equality of opportunity has not created an opportunity for equality. That is why we far prefer the idea of the maximization of possibilities.

The progressivism we seek to define is not an abstraction: it is a doctrine of political action. The principle of 'maximization of possibilities' must therefore find concrete expression. For this we have, as it were, to lift the bonnet of the car and get our hands inside the engine.

The cult of education rather than the cult of qualifications

The first step is, of course, education. There is no greater widening of 'possibilities' than teaching a child to read, write, think, be curious, behave, and have self-confidence. Education is what makes 'possibilities'... possible!

The mother of all battles for the progressivist is not the conquest of Mars or the solar system. It is the complete education of every person. This will require even more resources – for schools and universities, of course, but especially for continuing education. Ultimately, everyone should be able to return to training for a year, two years, or three years, so as to reorient themselves. This is indispensable economically: we are more and more frequently going to face changes of profession due to technological changes. But it is also essentially linked to our first principle: we must be able to 'reinvent ourselves' during our lives. What is the value of possibilities limited by the education you have received by the age of sixteen?

But the amount of public money spent on education is not the only factor determining success or failure. Recent research has shown that the rate of defaults on student debt will probably increase dramatically in the coming years.[1] Beyond the huge social problem this poses, what lesson can we draw? One conclusion is that the private sector does not fully value an educated population (in terms of culture, democratic life, etc.): in other words, some education is very useful to society, as it trains citizens to know about the history of their country, to master its language and become acquainted with some of its major political issues, but it is less useful to a company. So, we cannot rely solely on future salaries to pay for present studies, and additional public investment is necessary. But the gap between the cost of education and the salaries paid to graduates is so great that the content of what is taught probably does not live up to people's expectations and the efforts they put in. They pay a lot but they learn too little. It is a cruel reminder that educational investment is only useful if it is accompanied by a profound change in its nature and methods. This question has often been ignored, and it goes well beyond the United States. Let's look at the last decades. In most countries in the world, the duration of compulsory education has increased considerably. This is indisputably an advance. But in Western countries, it has become almost an end in itself, neglecting the central question that should have followed the growth of mass education at every stage: what do we actually want our children to learn and therefore how do we want our schools to teach?

France has undoubtedly been one of the biggest victims of this stunted vision of education. The traditional political parties in France have never wanted to engage seriously in this debate because, basically, they are not really interested in schooling as such: they are mainly interested in the qualifications one gets. They assume that access to qualifications determines access to employment and therefore one's entire social destiny. If the distribution of qualifications is fair, then society will also be fair. This is one of the many perverse effects of the misunderstanding over equality of opportunity. The result, to borrow the words of the France Stratégie think tank, is that 'the school system could be compared to a sports federation that organizes a competition by seeking mainly to ensure that the fields and rules of the game are the same for all, so that the outcome of the competition will be indisputable'.[2]

For left-wing parties, the biggest is that we will give too much help to the strongest (and therefore the wealthiest). For those on the left, a fair society involves equality at school; they are not so concerned with ensuring the true transmission of knowledge – even if this simply means being able to write correctly in adulthood. The only goal is to teach the same things to as many people as possible. 'We need to get 80 per cent of a generation as far as the baccalaureate', such a society proclaims, without wondering to what this qualification will actually give access. 'We need to smash elitism', it says, ruthlessly fighting to suppress anything that once allowed capable students to go further. Thus, on the pretext that Latin, for example, was a discipline that favoured the most favoured children, it was decided in France to close down a number of classes that taught it – as if it were not the greatest injustice to deprive future generations, especially those from working-class backgrounds, of a crucial instrument for understanding our culture and heritage.

For the right-wing parties, the biggest risk is, dare we say with some provocation, that, led astray by the left, we give too much help to the weakest (who are statistically the children from the poorest families). For those on the right, a fair society involves inequality at school. It must be acknowledged that the right has invested less politically in education than the left – perhaps because it sought fewer voters among teachers, or because its own children were not those most to be pitied. It therefore mainly defended the principle of selection and resisted aggressive efforts to impose a greater social mix or grant more resources to working-class schools.

These two attitudes are more complicit than they seem. Neither of them shows any interest in what's really happening in the classroom. And neither of them shows any interest in the many people who follow different paths.

The result of this lack of interest in the content and methods of teaching, a lack of interest found well beyond French borders, is that children have an increasingly utilitarian approach to school. They ask, 'What's the point?' They are bored, retain only what they need in order to pass exams and soon, once their professional life has begun, forget the essence of what they have learned. Only a small fraction of the population (and not only the richest or the most highly educated) will really have absorbed what they learned in the school system, and continue, for example, to read literature once they have left. The fetishism for exam results has emptied education of its entire substance, and there are more and more ghost classes in which teachers pretend to teach students who pretend to listen.

This state of affairs was already a social emergency. It has now become an economic emergency. You will no longer get a job in management unless you can speak foreign languages fluently and you will no longer get a job as a worker without mastering a whole range of ever more sophisticated technical skills and being able to adapt to technological changes and disruptions. You won't just be able to wave a diploma. Without a solid basis of knowledge, updated throughout life, many employees will be condemned to unemployment or underemployment. The entire country will then see its competitiveness collapse in the global race for innovation.

So, we need to make better use of the time we spend at school. For this reason, we need to abandon the cult of qualifications and replace it with the cult of education as such. We need to look again at what is happening in the classroom rather than in the exam room.

Many projects should emerge from a dialogue between teachers and educational theorists. Of one thing we are certain: the role of politicians is to organize this dialogue and to draw conclusions. They must not be obsessed by the duration or uniformity of teaching, but they must make sure that everyone learns as much and as well as possible – starting with those who have no other place to learn but school.

For instance, when you grow up in a cultivated family, you can ask your parents to help you to memorize, repeat, understand, and test yourself on what you have learned (most of the time you do not even have to ask). On the other hand, when you grow up in a less cultivated family, the school teacher is irreplaceable. This is why it is crucial, for example, to be able to do homework at school. In cases where pupils are the most autonomous, we can imagine taking things to their logical conclusion by completely reversing the situation: they will absorb lessons at home – thanks to digital technologies, all subjects are now available – and then practise in class what they have learned. We can consider going further: personalized learning adapted to each student, both in rhythm and method, could soon be offered, based on advances in artificial intelligence and big data.

In many countries, we also need to change the way people choose their courses. The educational system was first conceived to award places in a way that brooked no argument. For that, it was necessary to offer the same education to everyone up to a certain point and then ... it was too bad if it didn't work out. This is why we were not interested in the possibility that a student who had chosen a vocational path might later on feel drawn to a more general education if this ultimately answered his or her aspirations more fully. Let's return to the foundation of progressivism: possibilities. They differ according to people's talents and aspirations: we must allow each individual to reveal them, and thus offer a better adapted, less uniform education. To do the opposite is to store up trouble. But possibilities also change very quickly when you are young. People are not the same when they are fifteen as when they are twenty or twenty-five. So it should be possible to change course not once, but as many times as necessary. Instead of a uniform system, where it is difficult to change course, progressivists must work towards implementing a differentiated system where changing course is easy. Some countries, particularly in Northern Europe, are a good example to follow here.

Innovation versus monopoly

One might think that education brings two advantages. It opens our eyes to the world, and it should at the same time give us the material means to find our place in it – that is to say, first of all, a job. But education is not enough for people to obtain a job that will meet the progressivist demands for fulfilment, social utility and recognition, because the main structures of the economy serve an increasingly narrow minority, which monopolizes almost all the benefits of technological advances. If we do nothing, there is little reason why this should change.

The central economic question for progressivists is the diffusion of innovation. How can we ensure that its benefits are made available to everyone? This diffusion is not limited by technology – far from it! Today, technology can spread innovation at a marginal cost of almost zero. Much of the progress in computing is built on the open source model, where anyone can provide improvements in software for free. The enemy of the diffusion of innovation is monopoly – the artificial appropriation of innovation by a few big companies. The enemy of progressivists is monopoly rent. To quote J. E. Stiglitz putting all these sectoral evolutions in a broader perspective with regards to the United States: 'If monopoly power increases, monopoly profits will increase (...) But the productivity of the economy will decrease, and so too will the value of wages adjusted for inflation. Inequality will also increase.'[3]

Monopolies prevent innovation from being deployed in sectors of the traditional economy. Let's take the financial sector, for instance. Contrary to a widespread idea, finance in itself is very useful. But is it as useful for people that private banks should concentrate enormous power solely in their hands? We are indeed forced (or almost) to go through banks to make electronic payments; we are forced (or almost) to go through banks to obtain credit; we are forced (or almost) to go through banks to keep our savings safe. And so we are of course forced (or almost) to come to the aid of banks when they threaten to collapse. Major financial institutions are like a toll through which we are obliged to pass in order to gain access to economic life: they draw a considerable profit from this.

For decades, the main financial institutions have been engaged in increasingly aggressive and risky practices: we saw the result in 2008, when years of mistakes made in the financial sector nearly blew up the world's whole economic system. This is a well-established fact. Less well known is what economists Thomas Philippon[4] and Guillaume Bazot[5] have since revealed: for a century, whether in France, the United States, Germany or the United Kingdom, it has cost exactly the same amount to transfer a euro from the pockets of a saver into the pockets of a borrower – about two per cent. When you borrow at six per cent, two per cent goes solely into the pockets of the financial industry, just for putting investor and borrower in contact (without them even knowing about it), and four per cent to savers. What does the constancy of this figure reveal? That in a whole century there hasn't been the technological progress to enable funds to be allocated more quickly? That there has been no automation or computerization in the financial sector? Of course not. It simply means that this progress, instead of benefiting the whole population by reducing the costs of financial services, has benefited those major financial institutions alone; instead of serving the public interest, it has been used to fuel rents. Moreover, wages in the financial sector have rocketed over the past thirty years, so that this sector has attracted the most brilliant minds of the younger generations who would have often been more useful elsewhere.

The banks have been able to rely on a formidable ability for lobbying. The fact that they are huge, concentrated and vital to our economy gives them a political bargaining power that has no equivalent in other industrial sectors. Should we resign ourselves to paying undue taxes to rentiers? Finance costs too much – economically and politically. Thanks to new technologies, we can do better than just reform or regulate the traditional banking and financial sector (even though it is essential to do so): we can get around it.[6] All the ingredients are available. Thanks to the development of online banks, we will be able to secure our payments and use our accounts without paying excessive fees. With artificial intelligence, we will be able to borrow without the need to pay court to a bank advisor and without the risk of being taken for a ride. Thanks to the 'blockchain' – a system that certifies and secures transactions in a fully decentralized manner – we will certainly be able to raise funds or enter into complex and secured contracts without resorting to overpaid intermediaries. This is a struggle in which progressivists will have to engage for many years to come: they will need to prepare the framework for these innovations to unfold, and fight on behalf of actors who will be both safer and more innovative.

Progressivists are thus resolute enemies of the monopolies inherited from yesterday's world. But they will be just as fierce enemies of the monopolies of today's world. This is above all a question to be asked of the so-called GAFAM; that is, the main companies in the digital world (Google, Apple, Facebook, Amazon and Microsoft).

We explained in the previous chapter how they were naturally led to become monopolies: their value depends on their size. The more users they have, the stronger they are: eventually their power appears indestructible. Some might say, 'Where's the problem? These aren't your usual monopolies that, for lack of competition, impose excessive prices on the end consumer! On the contrary, the consumer pays nothing to use Google!' But Google is free only in appearance. Even if we don't pay a few pence every time we connect, we still pay for the growing digital monopolies in another and actually very expensive way.

The gigantic size of companies such as Google, Facebook, Amazon and Apple raises legitimate questions of sovereignty: any country might justifiably wish that such significant parts of the digital economy were not all American (or Chinese). The digital economy is no longer one sector among others, but the infrastructure on which our societies rely for their access to information and means of communication. Moreover, given the data that pass through our searches and digital interactions – data that will be used in every area – what we are dealing with is the raw material of our economy.

The huge size of such companies is already a problem for democracy. A single company cannot possess all the media of a country; this is a hangover from the time when people learned about the world from television or the press more than from the Internet. But can a single company be a hegemonic digital information platform for our fellow citizens in the way Facebook is about to become?[7] The algorithm for presenting and hierarchizing information can be made more or less fair: it will nonetheless remain true that a single algorithm decides what you can or cannot see, in the way a single official from the Propaganda Ministry would once have done. The public space must by definition belong to nobody: everyone can contribute to it, but no one should own it.

But beyond all these problems, progressivists are also sensitive to purely economic arguments. If these companies have access to a huge pool of data on which they can draw to offer ever more optimized services, and occupy a whole sector (online research, e-commerce, etc.), they also prevent their competitors from having access to these data and these sectors, slowing down the emergence of new players and new ideas, if necessary by mobilizing their considerable profits. In this respect, it is striking to see how much money these companies devote to buying up much smaller companies: this certainly makes it possible to offer very useful complementary services to the user, but it also makes it possible to avoid the rise of potential competitors. This is how Facebook bought Instagram in 2012: a billion dollars for a company that had about fifteen employees and hadn't a pennyworth of turnover. If Facebook had not done so, today we would have two rival social networks, allowing us to choose the one that best respects our privacy or offers the most practical use.

The nodal point of this approach is the issue of intellectual property, from the fruits of research and invention to the harvesting and optimization of data. These observations could equally well be applied to traditional industries which, by increasing the protection of patents, have succeeded in increasing their profits to the detriment of potential consumers and competitors.

For innovation to flourish, it must be rewarded, and therefore its inventors must be able to protect it for a sufficient period of time to make the necessary profit and to enable other individuals to be encouraged to become inventors as well. But for innovation to really maximize the 'possibilities' of all individuals, it must eventually be accessible, open, shared. There is only a knife-edge between these two imperatives. It involves using trade agreements to regulate global companies, rather than letting each country speak for 'its' monopolies internationally.[8] It involves redefining the doctrine of competition around the world. Many suggestions have already been made.[9] Should sanctions for concentration be tightened, including penalizing the bosses responsible? Should certain takeovers be prevented by GAFAM when they hamstring the development of potential competitors? Should we implement 'data portability' to enable us, for example, to migrate our list of contacts or our 'Facebook' data to other social networks that do not belong to that company, just as we can change our phone provider while keeping the same phone number?[10] All solutions must be clearly on the table – we should not be afraid to go as far as to dismantle these giants if necessary. The essential thing is to agree to establish a balance of power between global players. Admittedly, few states are able to stand alone against Google or Facebook – but on the scale of the European Union, the world's second largest economy, this becomes possible. The power of these digital giants is colossal – but a century ago the US federal government managed to dismantle Rockefeller's Standard Oil Company, whose annual turnover was then the equivalent of $1 trillion today, and which had blithely played fast and loose with the rules on competition enforced in different US states.

In economic terms, progressivists thus distinguish between the market economy, whose capacity for innovation, stimulated by competition, they acknowledge, and capitalism, which as they know tends towards concentration. They are therefore in principle on the side of the 'small' rather than the 'big'. Previously, they would have been on the side of Facebook when it was a young start-up, as against Rupert Murdoch, owner of one of the largest media groups in the world. Nowadays they are on the side of Qwant, the European search engine that respects your privacy, as against Google.

Positive discrimination is still discrimination

Freshening up the economy through innovation is not enough to maximize the possibilities of all individuals, as so many of them are stuck in initial situations from which there is no escape. If we take schooling and education out of the equation, since we talked about these earlier, there are still many obstacles in their paths, including one in particular: discrimination.

We immediately think of the discrimination that affects those who do not have the 'right' skin colour, of course – but we must not forget the discrimination against obese people and the disabled, or against people on grounds of their gender or their sexual orientation, or against those with a different accent or some other obvious idiosyncrasy. For all these victims, a schooling that gives them some self-confidence can really help, but the dismantling of industrial monopolies will not change anything. For decades, the only answer has been to debate the desirability of affirmative action – some have implemented it (e.g. in the United States); others have rejected it (especially in Europe). Neither of these two approaches has satisfactorily solved the problem of this hidden massacre of talents.

Above all, the positive discrimination approach poses two problems for progressivists. The first is that it amounts to turning the cause behind yesterday's discrimination into a reason for enjoying a better life tomorrow: it is because I am of African descent that, yesterday, I was unemployed; it is because I am of African descent that, tomorrow, I will be in work. This is inconsistent with the idea that everyone is entitled to be rewarded for their efforts, talents and merit. It is especially inconsistent with the idea that the maximization of possibilities mainly involves the desire not to be gauged all your life long by a characteristic that you have not chosen, or by which you refuse to be exclusively defined.

The second is that this approach is essentially statistical. Let's not even get into the debate of how to determine statistically who is from which ethnic background, or whether an individual is more homosexual than bisexual, or after which body mass index a person starts to be discriminated against because of his or her appearance ... Let's not even mention the competition for benefits that this would generate between more or less discriminated-against groups. Irrespective of this debate, which can easily be imagined as going on forever, the statistical approach is in essence contrary to progressivism, which targets individuals rather than reductive categories.

Positive discrimination is therefore not a progressivist tool. So what answer is there to the scourge of discrimination? After all, it drastically limits the prospects of so many individuals – a fact that usually meets with general indifference, since these same individuals are also relegated to the margins of the political system: they rarely vote, they are poorly represented and their voices are not properly heard.

We need, of course, to rely on the immediate tools of recruitment. All the structures (administrations, operators, companies) over which public authorities have power or influence should set an example. It's up to them to ensure that no candidate for recruitment will suffer any form of discrimination – starting from the very top, because an example is stronger the higher it is on the pyramid of power. Unfortunately, discrimination-free recruitment is a tool more talked about than used.

But we must above all create a sense of shame. Today's discrimination feeds on silence, hypocrisy and indifference: transparency can kill it. Those who have never been discriminated against feel personally uninterested in the subject and, above all, greatly underestimate the magnitude of the problem and the difficulties it poses for its victims. To put it another way, the main obstacle to solving the problem of discrimination is not that there is any passive resignation to the problem; it is that there is a profound ignorance of the existence of the problem itself. For example, we can bet that the vast majority of companies that engage in discrimination when hiring do so in an unconscious way: there is no instruction from the CEO, or from the Director of Human Resources, to sort out applications by physical appearance, religion, gender, and so on. Nonetheless, these applications are insidiously discarded as the process unfolds, for a variety of reasons related to habits, prejudices, risk aversion, and various cognitive biases that the behavioural sciences have clearly identified. This is why the first challenge of the progressivist when it comes to discrimination is to shine the spotlight on it wherever it occurs. Once there is consensus over the reality of the problem, the companies concerned will have no choice but to solve it – otherwise they will be exposed to the risk of a damaged reputation, loss of customers and public blacklisting. Very concretely, this means that the administrations in charge of the process must make it a priority of their public policies to organize mass testing campaigns. These consist of submitting fake applications that are perfectly equivalent except on the point suspected to be a source of discrimination, to see if the applicants are being treated fairly: the results should be fully published.

Tomorrow, augmented humanity?

How can progressivism enable us to anticipate the major ethical questions that will arise for us? Today, great advances in bio-medical techniques are opening up new perspectives, sometimes alluring, sometimes frightening. We will increasingly be able to go beyond simply 'healing' to 'augmenting' (our physical or cognitive abilities, even when we are in perfect health).

What, in this area, should be accepted, and what should be rejected? Answering this is well beyond the purpose of this book; but let us just state that 'maximizing possibilities' can in no way be interpreted as a blank cheque towards any phys-ically enhancing innovation. Some may provide short-term attractive gains, while corroding our humanity and reducing the 'possibilities' interpreted in a broader sense, by making our lives uniform, reducing our range of emotions, lessening the diversity of humankind, and so on. In fact, in our view, it is hardly fair to be expected to have a single opinion on all these issues – even though many in the public debate expect this. On the one hand, innovations can be of very different natures, and thus pose very different ethical questions: choosing, as if from a catalogue, the physical characteristics of our children; protect-ing ourselves better against diseases or infirmities; extending our healthy lives by thirty years, or significantly increasing our IQs, etc. On the other hand, we do not know exactly what, even in the very long term, is credible and what will always belong to science fiction. So we will need to examine, in each case, the reality and the substance of the actual possibilities, and the costs and losses they entail, without naivety or dogmatism.

Conversely, progressivism, as we have defined it so far, has something to tell us about the way to prepare for these debates. It has a general doctrine, which will brook no exception, and which must be affirmed as of today: these innovations, if they are ever authorized, will have to be placed at the service of all and not of a few. Imagine the opposite scenario – a world in which only a handful of individuals could extend their lives by a few decades by resorting to techniques too expensive for the rest of the population. Or imagine a world where only the wealthiest would be able to acquire a significant increase in their cognitive ability. A world in which some people possessed everything, from economic power to physical, intellectual and aesthetic domination, would undoubtedly be a nightmare for our democracy.

Proclaiming this principle of equality when it comes to accessing biotechnology is not the end of the debate on augmented humanity – it does not mean that an innovation is necessarily good once it is accessible to all: but it must be the prerequisite. It should now be written into our constitutions, to avoid our being overtaken by technological breakthroughs and presented with a fait accompli. To do so would serve a double purpose. First, it would avoid these innovations being gradually introduced by the elite, without a collective deliberation on their consequences. Second, it would ensure that even innovations that are deemed morally acceptable, or even desirable, by the public, are truly affordable to all, in order to avoid the frightening new age of inequalities that we have described above.

3

There are more possibilities when we act together (or the second principle of progressivism)

None of us knows what we all know together.

Euripides, 5th century BC

The reader who has followed us so far could argue that the progressivism we are trying to define is a new form of individualism, in which privacy is more important than community life, and in which it's fine to care little for others as long as they do not infringe on our rights to the 'pursuit of happiness' – in short, it's every individual for himself or herself, and there's nothing wrong with that. This is precisely what we do *not* mean by 'maximizing the possibilities'. On the contrary, it is because autonomy has been understood in this narrow form that it has not been realized for most people.

This individualistic conception was often promoted between the 1980s and the 2000s. It was believed that everyone's freedom was built *against* political power. Everything led people to be wary of the latter. The experience of totalitarianism encouraged people first and foremost to defend individual rights against the threats entailed by the state's pretensions to omnipotence; economic transformation needed to support innovation by leaving more room for entrepreneurial initiative; there were protests in the 1960s and later against a number of suffocating structures (the patriarchal family, the supervision of morals, the violence inflicted on certain minorities, and so on): all these factors mistakenly led people – especially in Europe – to see the national community and its patriotic expressions solely as the expression of a narrow-minded chauvinism.

This was an attack on common sense. We do not aspire to be mere isolated consumers. Neglecting the thirst for sociability and the aspiration to higher ideals would lead us to serious dead ends. We will come back to this later.

It was also a grave political misunderstanding. There is no real maximization of individual possibilities that does not depend on the maximization of collective possibilities. We do not have to choose between defending collective life and individual autonomy because we need the former if we are obtain the latter. Unless it draws on collective power, individual freedom is terribly diminished, and that is why the state did not stop growing as the individual continued to become more emancipated: this is not a contradiction in terms, quite the contrary – education, for example, is designed to emancipate the individual from baseless prejudices, to value merit against origin, to offer a horizon wider than one's home and hearth.[1] Social regulation has been designed to emancipate the individual from the hazards of fortune, the tyranny of the employer, excessive dependence on family and friends or those in one's immediate neighbourhood.[2] The majority of people cannot cope alone with insecurity, pollution or economic crises. And yet this is what has happened more and more since the 1970s.

The changes that have affected us most are the ones where political support has been most wanting. The result is that, since then, only those who have managed to play their cards right 'all by themselves' are really able to lead an independent life: when you are born in the right place, live in the right city, work for the right company with the right qualifications, your society offers you more opportunities – and more comforts – than any other in history. The frustration of those excluded is all the more intense. They call on the state for help, but the state has long since turned a deaf ear.

The sum of the possibilities of individuals who unite is thus worth more than the sum of the possibilities of each isolated individual. This is our second principle of progressivism: 'There are more possibilities when we act together.'

As we have forgotten this fact, we have relied for too long on wrongheaded generalizations. We thought that globalization necessarily implied that politicians no longer wielded much power: since the traditional nation-state was weakened, politics could no longer do anything. We thought that the cultural diversity of our societies necessarily implied growing fractures: the homogeneity of beliefs, origins and practices has been shaken by successive waves of immigration, so pride in belonging to the same country is outdated. We thought that growing individualization inevitably implied that individualism ruled: since everyone was henceforth free to pursue his or her own happiness, altruism and commitment are only fond but distant memories. In short, it was long thought that a person could only act alone, and henceforth only live separately. We will try to respond one by one to all these mistaken ideas.

Globalization without submission

We need, first and foremost, new tools to help us act. Let's look at the state of the political debate. Traditional parties have given up trying to tackle the most essential topics in our lives: the consequences of economic change for our societies, the impact of globalization on our territories, the transformation of our landscapes and the degradation of our health due to climate change and pollution. They have preferred to confront each other in media debates which, although important, are nonetheless secondary: a minor tax measure on good days, some vain controversy on bad ones. The long-standing intellectual and media consensus was that it was time to wave goodbye to political ambition: it was now impossible to influence the way the world was run – or at least, it was less possible than before. This is a lie – a convenient lie for some people but still a lie. It is true that we no longer have the institutions, at all levels, that would allow us to regain control of the ongoing transformations, but it is wrong to claim that we cannot rebuild them.

We can, for example, be more active at the local level.

We have allowed our daily lives to be reshaped by anonymous forces such as 'globalization' and 'metropolitanization', and by an increasing number of singular decisions, such as companies that keep moving their headquarters and public services that keep closing down. Entire regions where life used to be good have become quite inhospitable, from the American Midwest to South Australia, from the empty diagonal in France[3] to the Italian Mezzogiorno. Once prosperous boroughs have become ghost towns. In short, one essential transformation in our lives has not been the subject of any debate or discussion. But it is not inevitable. We saw in the previous chapter that opportunities of all kinds have been concentrated over time in a few unaffordable big cities, condemning the rest of the country to stagnation or decline. Of course, we need to encourage mobility and allow the maximum number of people to live where they can access the most possibilities, but that will not be enough. Not everyone is able or wants to live in one of the big cities. This is neither conceivable, as space is limited, nor desirable, since as the population increases, the quality of life deteriorates (congestion, pollution, etc.); it is not even inevitably desired, since not all Americans want to live in San Francisco or New York – thank goodness. As far as the rest are concerned, we need to fight against geographical inequalities by pursuing a policy of basically geographical redistribution.

This redistribution may be financial. Taxation, for example, generally aims to reduce income inequality (at least in Europe) – we pay higher or lower taxes depending on whether we are more or less rich. But it does not take into account geographical inequalities, which are embodied in the inequalities of access to real estate: in the metropolis, prices have soared – elsewhere, they have often collapsed. As we have seen, access to real estate is strategic because it is more than just a source of income: it opens – or closes – access to the best schools, the best companies, and so on. You should pay far fewer taxes when you own a house in the Midlands or Detroit than when you own an apartment in London or Manhattan. This system would facilitate mobility; it would also redistribute wealth and encourage people to live outside the big cities. French citizens, for example, used to pay a local tax ('taxe d'habitation') to finance the expenses of the municipality where they lived; this tax was often higher when the town was poorer and therefore lacked other resources. This was experienced as a great injustice: everyone knew that you paid a third as much tax in the centre of Paris than a hundred kilometres away, even though salaries in Paris were higher. Emmanuel Macron gradually eliminated this tax, implementing an unprecedented geographical redistribution, with a GDP point of tax cuts aimed principally at the most struggling areas.

This redistribution can also be political and symbolic, especially in countries where the capital city concentrates within itself a particularly large number of public institutions, as is the case in the United Kingdom or France. Compare the situation with Germany: is it legitimate for the Bank of France and the Bank of England to be in Paris and London when the Bundesbank is in Frankfurt? Is it necessary for the Constitutional Council to be located opposite the Louvre, and the House of Lords next to Big Ben, when the German Constitutional Court sits in Karlsruhe? Not to mention universities, publically owned companies and ministries ... Relocating them would be a significant move: it would have an immediate effect in terms of jobs, an important symbolic resonance, and a knock-on effect on the private sector.

It's not just about shaking things up across the country. It's a matter of allowing each village, each city, each region, to take more of its own destiny in hand. It is possible to give local solidarity the power it used to have.

Take the example of local currencies, which supplement national currencies by circulating only in small territories, where they make it possible to buy a limited range of goods while respecting such criteria as local production. There are said to be more than five thousand of these currencies across the world.[4] They are often in too rudimentary a form, which is a pity, because whenever you use one of these currencies you can be sure that the main beneficiary will be a trader or a producer from that area. They support the relocation of activity (jobs, local commerce, local knowledge), by encouraging people to buy from local service providers, who themselves buy from local suppliers, rather than using, for example, euros to shop in supermarkets for products transported from thousands of kilometres away. This is good industrial policy because it stimulates the development of relations between companies that are geographically close; it's good economic policy, because it gives better support to local demand in a crisis; and it's good environmental policy, because it does not rely on long journeys. But, at present, national regulatory frameworks too often prevent these local currencies from developing. Why not at least help local authorities to support their development, for example by allowing them to pay their expenses and collect their taxes in local currency, as a reasonable proportion of their budget? The United Kingdom has gone far in this direction.

Local territory has been progressively equipped with means of defence (*appellation contrôlée*, protected designation of origin, protected areas, etc.) to ward off irrational globalization. It's now time to provide it with the means of attack.

We can also be more active on the continental scale. Trade and the movement of capital have put paid to the idea of fully autonomous national economic policies. Geopolitical inter-dependencies have put paid to the idea of fully autonomous migration policies. The same could be said about matters of security, research and science. In the same way that individuals have an interest in cooperating, states must also understand that they can do more together than in isolation.

Let's take an example. Economists generally agree that, at the level of society as a whole, trade produces a net gain: trade enriches us. More specifically, some companies are winners and others losers, but there are more winners than losers. Ideally, we should redistribute wealth from the former to the latter (for example, by compensating the unemployed and helping them move from declining sectors to more prosperous sectors). The only problem is that 40 per cent of the profits of multinational firms are made in countries where taxation is low or zero:[5] winners win but they pay nothing! The issue needs to be addressed at the global level. This is not a utopian desire, and significant progress has already been made at the OECD level. Technical solutions are available. The economist Gabriel Zucman, for example, suggests taxing companies in accordance with the country where they make their sales rather than where they declare their profits. Optimization would no longer be possible, and companies would no longer be interested in locating themselves, in fact or fiction, in countries where tax rates are lower. Other options can be defended, but the essential point remains: acting alone means that you aren't acting at all.

It is in response to the way states have been weakened by growing interdependence that the need for Europe must be understood. It is not a question of arbitrarily imposing Brussels' preferences on Europeans, but of identifying the points where we all have an interest in grouping together so as to have a bigger impact at the global level. This does not mean abandoning sovereignty but increasing it. The European Union is not in competition with individual nations but at their service.[6] We are not talking about a struggle that should ultimately end in the disappearance of the EU or of individual nations: this is the mistake made both by so-called 'federalists' and by those who proclaim themselves to be 'sovereignists'. It is not a European supra-nation that we want to build, but a Europe of super-nations.

So how is it that the European debate is mired in apparently insoluble difficulties? If the way forward were so easy, so obvious, why has our generation always criticized or decried the EU, and seen it as always on the verge of crisis? Why does every proposal for pooling resources to tackle economic problems, immigration and security become the subject of fierce disputes that ultimately lead, most of the time, to lukewarm compromises with which nobody is entirely happy?

The first problem faced by pro-Europeans is that they have long projected a simplistic ideal onto the European Union, envisioning it as a unitary, uniform structure that applies the same rules to all member states. The enemy was an 'à la carte' Europe. Of course, exceptions have been made, but they were narrow in scope or applied only for a limited period. It was still taken for granted that you could take everything from Europe, or nothing. The result is that the decision has increasingly been to take nothing. Nations wishing to pool their strengths in one area or another have been blocked by those who are more cautious.

But it needs to be stated that, in key areas where a particular group of countries want to go further, they should be able to do so without waiting for others and without being subject to their veto. If the European Union is not a super-state, then it does not need to work as a single bloc. There could be one group of countries that decides to pool its monetary policy (this group already exists), another that decides to have a new defence policy, and a third that has its own policies on asylum. Each domain would of course have its specific rights and duties.[7]

The second problem that pro-Europeans face is that it is very difficult for governments to abandon the prerogatives they have exercised for decades, if not for centuries. This is sometimes for bad reasons – they are simply afraid of losing the privileges of power – but sometimes for good reasons. Germany fears that the pooling of financial resources, essential to the smooth functioning of the single currency, may simply mean it squanders its wealth to help irresponsible states: it must be patiently convinced that a prosperous Eurozone will benefit all, including the Germans, and that all states will need to behave responsibly.

Italy fears that the pooling of immigration policies may simply transform it into a gigantic refugee camp: it must be patiently convinced that the joint protection of borders will benefit all, including the Italians, and that all states will have to play their part in the reception of migrants entitled to asylum. Ireland fears that the pooling of tax policies will simply undermine its economic advantage, which lies in providing foreign companies with very low tax rates: it must be patiently convinced that this advantage is only a short-term one and will eventually lead to the weakening of all. So we need to be patient as we win over the member states, one by one: this is an indispensable, often exasperating and always interminable process. Sometimes, it's impossible. Often, breakthroughs are made in times of intense crisis.[8] That is why it is so crucial to be able to reverse the functioning of the European Union: to move from the current situation in which the rules allow any member state to block all the others to a situation in which no country will be able to stop others from moving faster.

Over and above these institutional considerations, the second mistake of the European Union is that it has not gone much faster when it was in a position to do so – in areas where states have no, or few, prerogatives. This is the case, for example, with technological progress: all governments take it for granted that we have no control over major waves of innovation; for example, those based on the development of digital technology, robotics or (more recently) artificial intelligence. If luck is on our side, they will create jobs and protect our privacy. If not, they will destroy the middle classes and subject our existence to the diktat of algorithms. Yet these innovations do not grow like mushrooms: they are invented by human beings. But these human beings do not always have the general European interest in mind. For example, we are beginning to see how artificial intelligence is going to revolutionize urban life. In China, artificial intelligence is used to identify each individual at every moment, so as to exert on him or her a social control (or worse) that has no precedent in the history of humanity. If you cross a road without using a pedestrian crossing, you'll see your face and name flashing up on all the digital display panels in the neighbourhood (it is likely that the information collected will also be used to 'rate' the behaviour of individuals and identify those who may be less likely to respect the Chinese regime's strict rules). In Europe, we are working more on the anonymous use of artificial intelligence: when we know for example that so many cars pass by a particular junction at a particular time of the day, causing daily traffic jams, then we can develop transport alternatives to free up the public roads. The European Union has the means and the skills to forge the artificial intelligence that Europeans want, rather than to have to bow down to the artificial intelligence they do not want: it should seize this opportunity before it's too late.

The third problem facing pro-Europeans is that it is very difficult for people to accept transfers of sovereignty. Why? Partly because they fear that this will translate into less responsiveness. They think we won't have as much hold on officials in Brussels as we do on officials in Paris, Rome or Berlin. This is true, and to some extent it's inevitable: an election in a single state cannot by itself call into question the decision of an entity that represents nearly thirty states. So, what Europe does cannot be undone by one of its members, unless it wants to leave the Union.

The mistake of the European Union is that it has not been able to accept this side of things. If the European Union focuses on long-term issues such as technological progress and the environment, and on compromises patiently reached between states as regards migration and the economy, it is obvious that it won't be able to respond quickly. But this weakness can be a force. It helps Europe to set a course at a time when national democracies are struggling to build projects that will take ten or twenty years. The European Union must make it possible to protect choices that embody a whole civilization against more short-sighted decisions: it isn't possible to govern an environmental policy, or ponder profound issues such as research into artificial intelligence, by annual elections (if elections in each member state are taken into account). For a long time, it has been argued that, in order to restore Europe's prestige, it must be given small-scale but positive issues to deal with. We claim the opposite. We must let Europe take on big issues, even if it makes itself temporarily unpopular: it is at this price that it will show its worth, a worth that goes beyond that of merely national governments. Slower responsiveness, of course, doesn't mean less accountability: all these policies will be controlled by the citizens, first and foremost in European elections.

One issue, for example, needs to be tackled at European level: the 'decarbonization' of our economies and our societies. Europe must become the 'carbon fund' of its twenty-seven member states, gradually taking charge of major decisions in this area (whether tax or support costs). We will come back to this in our fourth chapter.

Diversity without division

However, it is not always enough to have the right tools. Before we can *act* together, we must already *want* to be together. It's good to praise diversity. But the truth is that the closer we are, and the more we resemble each other, the more we trust each other. And the more we trust each other, the more we want to act in common. Our societies are incorporating ever more people with different origins, beliefs and attitudes. In fact, a more homogeneous society and a more heterogeneous society both have positive and negative traits, and the challenge of our times is to take the best of both.[9]

This raises a lot of political questions that irritate people; this is natural because they are difficult questions. Let's try to apply to them our first two principles of progressivism.

First, let's think about immigration. We have the right – not only juridically but morally – to choose who joins the 'national community'. Let's conduct an argument *ad absurdum*. Imagine opening up our borders. It is quite obvious that the first thing that would disappear would be our ability to act together – we wouldn't know each other, we wouldn't trust each other. The great waves of immigration to the United States in the nineteenth century were possible only because the American state advocated a radical individualism and had a vast and very sparsely populated territory. Only a few extremist groups want there to be 'no borders'. So, once the right to asylum is accepted, everyone agrees on the need to establish criteria for admission to the community of citizens. But the left, including in its more moderate expressions, has too often restricted the legitimate criteria to those of an economic and social nature: the state of the labour market or of housing. It is crucial to add a political criterion: the willingness to act with others, to adopt principles, to support the common project. Patriotism is not, for the progressivists, an archaism: on the contrary, it is an essential feeling if we are to be properly concerned by the future of our national community, and thus to contribute to it. It would be quite wrong to abandon it to other political or social groups. It must be cultivated in those who are already citizens, and demanded from those who aspire to become citizens.

This also raises the religious question. While faith is an intimate affair, religions are a social affair, affecting our daily practices, our interpersonal relationships, our behaviour in the world. However, what we are witnessing at present is really a resurgence of manifestations of belonging, evident in whatever country or religion – for while people talk a great deal about Islam in this respect, a renewed intensity can be also observed in Christianity and Judaism.

Progressivists must answer this question, relying on their first two principles as a moral compass. No more and no less is required. No more: for any arbitrary hierarchy of identities or civilizations is foreign to them, and it is completely absurd and dangerous to assert the intrinsic superiority of one identity over another, one religion over another, or even of atheism over faith (or the other way around). No less: for there is no reason not to subject religious ideologies to the same scrutiny as secular ideologies, and to critique practices inspired by adherence to a religious dogma in the same way as practices inspired by adherence to a political doctrine.

Progressivists are therefore neither for nor against religions. They think that these should be given a place within a definite framework. This framework should first and foremost ensure that religions do not reduce the possibilities of individuals. This implies that everyone can freely choose his or her religion. Here we need the law, as it protects the freedom *not* to believe. We know that the family, neighbours and classmates can exert a very strong pressure on children, who do not yet have the capacity to choose their convictions autonomously, and impose a certain practice on them: children must be protected, especially at school. France, for example, has decided to ban religious signs from schools, to provide a space for indeterminacy. This is why progressivists must always be on the side of freedom of expression, without which there is no freedom at all: they do not believe in blasphemy, and so they are always on the side of cartoonists, whether the latter are funny or not. But the law also protects the freedom to believe, because we also know that some use secularism as a weapon against Islam, to prevent its faithful from living freely and to preserve a certain idea of their country. In France, this idea is White and Christian. No slide into this tendency can be tolerated. This is why progressivists are not in favour of the prohibition of religious symbols at university, as some French MPs have suggested: this would amount to placing illegitimate limits on the right to practise one's religion.

In short, progressivists are defenders of secularism, one that guarantees the freedom to believe and not to believe. This is one place where France is really exemplary. Secularism is not an archaism, or a piece of national folklore. On the contrary, it is a tremendously powerful tool to preserve individuals' autonomy in the face of pressures of all kinds.

Once this framework is respected, once we have ensured that religious affairs do not jeopardize everyone's possibility to choose their life, then we can look at the second principle: how to combine religions with the possibility of acting together?

To collaborate, individuals need to have shared cultures, reference points and passions. When, long ago, religions were practised in a relatively uniform way throughout a particular country, they formed the cement of society. Today, in most Western countries, they are much more diverse and operate in a much more fragmented manner: they can, indeed, isolate their followers from the rest of society. Combining them with shared actions has therefore become more problematic, and creates a great deal of perplexity in everyday life: this is a matter that needs careful, case-by-case consideration.

In schools, for example, religion has triggered many debates in several European countries. Should we reschedule an examination when it falls on a major Jewish or Muslim holiday? What food should be served in canteens when some pupils do not eat pork? Should we allow mothers who wear the veil to accompany their children on school outings? Provided that the first principle of progressivism is not violated, the role of the state is to do everything possible to foster a spirit of 'fraternity', and thus allow the second principle to be applied. That is why, if progressivists are very firm in their desire to ban religious symbols in schools, they find it absurd not to allow alternatives to pork to be served in canteens: we ought to be happy that children can sit together at the same table, whatever the convictions of their families. Similarly, progressivism should not judge it advisable to forbid veiled mothers from taking part in public school outings: on the contrary, we should welcome the fact that different religious groups can send their children to the same school and that everyone can associate with the life of the establishment. Common sense is often quite enough to overcome these pseudo-problems that the most irresponsible political leaders like to blow up out of all proportion.

On the other hand, we feel that it is legitimate to ban the wearing of the burqa or niqab in all democracies. For, by completely covering their faces, the niqab does not allow women to take part in shared communications. It thus profoundly offends our sense of collective life. Imagine a society where all women wore the burqa: half of humanity would then be cut off from public space and from the ability to act with others!

It is therefore with these two priorities in mind that progressivism must address the religious question. Progressivism guarantees the freedom to believe and not to believe, and if necessary it does so by passing laws. It promotes daily life between people of different origins and convictions. Of course, the questions posed by diversity cannot be reduced to questions about immigration or religion. But these are the thorniest problems, and that's why we took them as an example.

Progressivism must in fact, always and everywhere, demonstrate a form of civic politeness. This means paying more attention to what brings us together than to what divides us. This applies to the differences of other people: this is what people on the right in particular find it difficult to understand. They are too eager to distance themselves, to point the finger at those who stand out, to stir up quarrels of identity and endless divisions. But this also applies to oneself: this is what people on the left in particular find it difficult to understand. We can't always foreground our particularities without sooner or later fracturing our capacity to live and act together.

The individual without individualism

The increasing importance of the idea of autonomy has rid us of many stifling ideologies. We can now exist for ourselves, reject the roles we were assigned, try to shape society in accordance with our aspirations and our self-images. We no longer need to seek death on the battlefield in wars waged at the whim of sovereigns: never again will we be fodder for the cannons. We no longer need to seek salvation by living in the shadow of churches, mosques or synagogues: never again will we be fodder for dogmas. We need no longer abandon our critical sense and serve some charismatic leader: never again will we be fodder for political parties. This has not been the case for everybody, of course, but it has applied to a growing majority.

But this progress went astray, and we lost many of those places where we could act in the service of ideals which, surpassing each of us individually, united us all. We have in mind both the 'great' ideals, those which united citizens called up to fight for their country, faithful worshippers in the village, party comrades, and 'little ideals' such as disinterestedness and generosity that kept neighbourhoods alive. These ideals meant that we knew we were not alone. They encouraged everyone to commit to the good of the community.

We insist on the loss of *places* because, contrary to what some conservatives believe, the fact that commitment is no longer imposed does not mean that it is unthinkable. Just as the disappearance of traditional family authority has not suppressed solidarity and affection between parents and children, the disappearance of many traditional places in which commitment was expressed has not eliminated the desire for such commitment. These elements are too deeply rooted in human nature. The desire for commitment is still there – as evidenced by the dynamism of voluntary associations and the effervescence of social networks – but it often does not know how to express itself. We need to rediscover it in all its power, because there are many causes that deserve to be fought for, starting with the defence of your country when it is threatened.

Efficiency itself dictates this, even outside periods of general mobilization in wartime. Citizens who play a part in the life of their society can achieve more than any law or government.

The role of the public authorities is to enable these citizens to act.

It's easy to wax indignant about things these days – you need only watch the news on television. But once the news has been absorbed, we quickly move on to something else, instead of severely punishing the intolerable behaviour that has been reported; and we end up resigning ourselves to seeing failing bosses leaving with golden handshakes, and very senior executives in protected jobs being awarded huge salaries. But isn't it the state's job to act? Sometimes, but not always. We will never be able to make a 'fair wage' an integral part of the law: it is absurd to point an accusing finger at the entrepreneur who makes a fortune by setting up a company, or the footballer or the basketball player who makes a fortune by nourishing the daydreams of millions of people. There is only one constraint that is both fair and effective, because it trusts to everyone's individual judgement to treat each situation appropriately, namely social constraint. In the case of a company that is misbehaving, for example, small shareholders should refuse to invest, banks should refuse to lend, customers should refuse to buy its products, etc. What is the role of the public authorities? To allow this constraint to be exercised. For that, information is required. How much do the leaders of this company earn? What is the pay structure? From which branch or factory do the most significant profits come? These are the sinews of war: we must not force companies to do things differently – but we must compel them to say loud and clear what they *do* do. The company can no longer be judge and jury. The citizens must be judges.

Commitment is effective, but above all it is exhilarating. It is not a question of knowingly calculating how much to sacrifice, hoping that the material profits will live up to expectations.

In reality, we do not always diminish ourselves when we devote ourselves to a collective task: on the contrary, we diversify our possibilities by accessing a singular type of happiness, different from that which a strictly individual experience provides.[10] We have all encountered such moments of satisfaction: participating in a summer camp with young people from all across the US, organizing a fundraiser for an NGO (despite the refusals and the sarcastic put-downs), yielding to the urge that makes us train for hours in a football or baseball stadium so our team will win (despite the pelting rain), the thrill of being at a political meeting or in a packed concert hall. Those who have belonged to an organization – whatever its purpose – are familiar with the particular feeling that is not friendship (it is less intimate) nor a professional relationship (it is less cold) – the feeling of camaraderie. This fraternity unites us by giving us the sense of participating in something greater than ourselves.

This is why the thirst for commitment can lead to anything. It led hypnotized young people to applaud the Nazi hordes, and other young people to fight for so-called Islamic State. We should not deny this thirst for commitment, and above all not try to extinguish it, but use it for the best.

Thus, the commitment for which we call does not conflict with the first principle of progressivism. It maximizes the possibilities of individuals in two senses. First of all, commitment is an instrument: it allows us to act together, thus ultimately increasing everyone's range of possibilities. Second, it is an end in itself: it makes us participate in more or less disinterested actions which in themselves provide us with an intense feeling of fulfilment.

Western societies are often accused of having a 'symbolic void' at their hearts. By sending everyone off to pursue their own happiness, they create shrunken lives and neurotic individuals, and there is truth in this denunciation. But we do not believe that it is necessary to repopulate the Earth with myths, or to invent a new 'political religion' after the hundreds of these that have driven individuals and peoples, very often to disappointment if not to disaster. It is said that developed societies are the 'orphans of an ideal': we think that human beings themselves are an ideal, and that enabling them to find self-fulfilment is a sufficiently revolutionary ideology to foster commitment. But if the human being is an ideal, we do not think that everyone can be his or her *own* ideal. Instead, we believe in the individual without individualism.

This is the heart of what distinguishes progressivism from liberalism. Admittedly, we are in a way pursuing the same goal (the empowerment of the individual) and we share a certain number of means (confidence in individual initiative enlightened by reason and supported by science). This explains why we have had, and still have, many shared fights on our hands. But we diverge on essential points. The fundamental maxim of liberalism is: 'Everyone should seek his or her personal interests, institutions should protect fundamental rights, and the result will be the greatest good for the greatest number.'

On the contrary, we think that the general interest does not stem from some blind game. Capitalism can apportion goods in an absurd way when it comes to maximizing possibilities, crushing some people and giving too much to others. This is why we believe in public investment, in a relentless fight against rent and in a certain degree of redistribution: this was the topic of the previous chapter. That's why we also believe in political action, which allows us to shape the blind forces that are too often seen as unstoppable – that's what we've seen in connection with globalization and the question of national territory.

But even more fundamentally, we believe that no one can be reduced to a being of pure egoism, maximizing his or her well-being at each moment. However, albeit in a more vulgar form than that elegantly promoted by liberal philosophy, the idea has spread that everyone should be content to earn the maximum amount of money – something that would buy not only a really nice house, but also the respect and even affection of his or her friends and acquaintances. This ethics leads society to disaster. Of course, the money we earn and the consumption it makes possible will always be a determining factor in our satisfaction. But if these are the only goals that we pursue, then we will be caught in a terrible trap, as we all seek constantly to increase our profits in an endless race where we will exclude others and eventually destroy ourselves.[11]

It is to break out of this vicious circle that we must first find the means to act by creating institutions adapted to the new worlds we live in, from the most local to the most international, so that globalization will not involve mere passive submission.

Then, we must find the capacity to live together, to form a community (a *political* community), defending a diversity without division: we have talked about what this implied in terms of vigilance when it comes to immigration and religion. Finally, we must support the will to act of individuals by cultivating the sense of commitment and creating an individual without individualism. But how, precisely, are we to do this?

4

Starting from the bottom (or the third principle of progressivism)

We now come to an essential point: the method of public action. Traditionally, in books about politics, this is dealt with in a few lines of key words: 'open' methods, 'cooperation', 'assessment', 'participatory democracy'. Communication, the political programme: these are noble matters. The rest is considered to be humdrum, routine work: an unavoidable add-on.

Such a conclusion would be a fatal mistake. It is more difficult for progressivists to exercise power than to win it. Once they have started to tackle their responsibilities, stagnation lurks on every side, since everything is organized to manage the existing state of affairs and not to transform it. Why? Because power structures have changed little in recent decades. They are arranged in the same pyramid shape. At the top, at the very top, is a head or leader (of state, community, etc.). Under this leader come 'mediating bodies', that is to say structures which, as their name suggests, are responsible for the interface between the leader and the citizen. And at the bottom we find the multitude of anonymous citizens. As one goes upwards, the mediating bodies are supposed to transmit desiderata from the base to the leader. And, as one goes downwards, the same bodies should apply and forward the leader's decisions to the base.

This is the challenge of our time. The appetite for commitment is still there, but it is no longer satisfied with the old structures. As a result of raising the level of education, we want our singular voices to be heard, whether as activists, trade unionists or civil servants, and we want more freedom in the exercise of our responsibilities – overly pyramidal organizations seem stifling. As a result of digital technologies, we can now allow citizens to self-organize much more easily – overly pyramidal organizations seem inefficient. Entire sections of society have understood this revolution, but it has not penetrated into political life.

Politics must first learn to look down. Each higher echelon should consider how to increase the possibilities of the lower echelons, while of course guaranteeing that their actions are consistent. It should set a course and then give the means to reach its goal, with everyone being responsible for attaining it. This is our third and final principle of progressivism: 'start from the bottom'. The pyramidal way in which political power is thought of in our societies must therefore be radically reversed.

All this may seem excessively abstract, or simplistic. And yet, this model actually explains why many organizations essential to the good functioning of democracy (administrations, unions, local authorities, political parties) are in crisis, and provides solutions.

The new administration

Administration has played a key role in embodying and implementing the general interest. Properly spurred on by political will, it has achieved extraordinary things, such as sending a man to the moon in America in the 1960s and reuniting the two Germanys after 1989. Since then, its size has not diminished. In the European Union, for example, almost half of all wealth goes into taxes – this is also the case for a quarter of the wealth produced in the United States or South Korea, and almost a third of that produced in Japan. Yet we have the impression that elections and laws have lost much of their ability to change our lives. Paradoxically, we are under the impression that the increase in size has come with a decrease in power. Some of this has to do with the spectacular changes our societies underwent during the 'globalization' era and we have already referred to those. But we would like to highlight a different aspect of things, an organizational issue. This is a high priority for us because, in our view, all the dangers that currently threaten politics (the rise of extremists, the disaffection of citizens, conspiracy theorists, etc.) are mainly attributed to the impotence of politicians: in whatever country, things change too little and too slowly in the eyes of its citizens, despite repeated promises made by all newly elected govern ments. More precisely, the difficulty comes from the way decision-implementing is organized: there is a 'black hole' between the passing of a law, however well designed, and the transformation of everyday life. Too few people are held accountable for concrete implementation.

Elected officials seek to make a name for themselves and look exclusively forward, never backwards. Ministers or MPs dream of making headlines and of being associated with the passing of new laws. What happens next – the implementation and application, the corrections to be made and the results to be obtained – is secondary: the news chases after the real. The upper levels of the administration follow along in the train of emergencies, as much as they can. As for the rest of the public service, busy with the usual tasks, feeling under-recognized and undervalued, it casts a cautious gaze at the avalanche of instructions thundering down on top of it.

How can all this be changed?

First, by appointing fully responsible ministers. These days, the state regulates so many domains that it often merely replicates the contradictions of society instead of solving them. Officials in the department of agriculture traditionally oppose those in the department for the environment, officials responsible for work and pensions oppose those at the Department of the Interior, and so on. And let's not even mention the more or less open conflicts that often pit ministers themselves against each other! However, almost all of the major issues that we face today concern at least two departments. Immigration management? It's the business of both the Department of the Interior and the Department of Foreign Affairs. The environment? It falls under the ministry of the same name, but also involves the departments of transport, agriculture, etc. Bringing down unemployment? This involves the Ministry of Finance, the Ministry of Education, and so on. We can add to these examples almost indefinitely: we have created ministries in accordance with the administrations they oversee, and not with the mandate they were given by the electorate. This leads the state at best to make lame compromises, and at worst to paralysis. On the contrary, we should appoint ministers not as heads of administration, but as project leaders, according to the political priorities of the moment: a minister in charge of reducing unemployment; a minister in charge of immigration and integration; a person responsible for switching from cars to less polluting vehicles; with authority over the administrations concerned where necessary. This could solve coordination issues and refocus part of the government on its core mandate. It would also allow for greater accountability. At the end of the time allotted, it would be easy to measure the success or otherwise of the mission, and to draw the necessary consequences: the leader would be replaced, promoted to a more important post, granted an extended period in office, and so on. The daily management of things would be in the hands of a more classic type of minister, or even in the hands of highly competent civil servants, as long as close scrutiny by Parliament were ensured.

Second, the administrative culture needs to be changed. Contrary to popular belief, one that is particularly deeply rooted in France, the quality of an administration is not measured primarily by that of its senior officials, but by that of its field agents. What matters isn't the administration in Washington, but the administration in Detroit or Baltimore. Its mission is to serve citizens: the most important tasks are those that lead to direct contact with ordinary people. This should be self-evident, and it explains why, in the radically new administration that we call for, it's the senior civil servant who should serve the public official out in the field, and not the other way round. The former should spend his or her days wondering how the latter can be helped to improve his or her actions. And every minister must do the same with senior civil servants.

Public officials must be made both more autonomous and more responsible: they must focus on aims, not means. They must therefore be given a proper hearing on how to concretely implement decisions. On the other hand, they must be held accountable for both positive results and failures in their area of concern, applauded for the former and penalized for the latter. The challenge is not only to apply the measures passed by Parliament, but to ensure that they are used, that they produce the desired effects, that they are useful, that they transform reality. All too often, a field agent applies instructions from above without being able to adapt them to the difficulties he or she encounters; the senior civil servant applies the laws passed by Parliament without feeling responsible for their outcome, and without making every effort to ensure that they work. And then the minister discovers, a few months later, that the reform he or she thought was revolutionary has not even been really implemented. The result? Civil servants who find little meaning in their jobs, governments which think that the administration is torpedoing its projects, and citizens who believe that politics is now quite incapable of changing their lives.

The new mediating bodies, the new local democracy

For centuries, mediating bodies have played a tremendously useful role, keeping society peaceful, supporting the modernization of the economy, developing different sectors (for example, unions, professional bodies, groups of local elected representatives, chambers of commerce and industry, etc.). But this role is now being called into question, for one obvious reason: there are very simple ways of getting by without any mediating step between the base and the summit. The cost of transmitting information, whether upwards or downwards, is almost nil. If you want to express your discontent, for example, there's no need to join a union, to campaign for years, to accept compromises, to submit to its leadership: in a few days, thanks to social networks, millions of citizens who share the same view can be assembled. The main raison d'être of mediating bodies is therefore undermined, as was the case, in other domains, with water carriers when plumbing was invented, or taxis when applications such as Uber and Blacklane were created, or hotels when rental platforms between individuals became a possibility.

Does the solution consist in simply avoiding any mediating, by creating channels of direct two-way communication between a leader and the people? This is often suggested by those who favour the drift into authoritarianism currently affecting many countries, and rely on a formidable personality cult. This works because the relevant intermediaries have actually become impotent, as all can see. But it is particularly dangerous because, when other powers are destroyed, it is freedom that is restricted and democracy that is weakened. In accordance with our second principle, it is vital to allow individuals to organize and set out structures outside the exclusive sphere of the state – structures that will allow them to act together.

The current mediating bodies (associations of local elected representatives, unions, etc.) must regain their legitimacy by starting from the bottom, rather than by handing down instructions from above. Individuals have grown tired of seeing this mode of operation produce only an insidious form of collective impotence; they lose interest in mediating bodies, which end up no longer being able to mediate at all. They should therefore stop exclusively focusing their efforts on how best to convince the state to take a certain decision. Instead, they should directly help citizens transform their businesses and their neighbourhoods, preserve their environment, and so on. In a nutshell: they, too, must start again from the bottom. For instance, municipalities are particularly affected by this new availability of information.

Of course, there are serious reasons to show strong support (as against those who favour 'direct democracy' at every level of government) for representative democracy, both national and European. The seriousness and complexity of the issues make it essential to elect representatives who will devote all their time and resources to taking decisions for whose effects and coherence they will accept responsibility.

On the other hand, these arguments are often less convincing when one looks at the more local scale. Political action at this level takes place on a human scale, and elected representatives are in direct contact with their constituents, who can see for themselves, month by month, the results of their action. And digital tools offer new perspectives. The result? There is much more room for direct consultation.

It is obviously a complicated matter – if not impossible – to bring together all the residents of a small town, in France or elsewhere, so they can vote regularly on a programme put forward by the mayor. How is one to ensure, month after month, that enough citizens will make the trip? How will a big enough infrastructure be found? How can one give the debate time to unfold so that people can ponder the issues? The risk is that the consultations will be monopolized by a very highly motivated minority of the population: this is what has been observed in many municipalities where consultations on budgetary constraints have been organized, particularly after the experiments conducted in Brazil. Digital technology can reduce this risk: one can well imagine many of the deliberations of municipal councils being subject to direct voting (online, but also physically, for those who do not have access to such instruments) on the part of the residents of the municipality concerned, over a sufficient period of time for as many people as possible to participate.

Better still, there is no justification for elected officials being solely able to put forward proposals concerning the whole municipality. It would be technically easy, and politically legitimate, to allow a number of citizens representing a sufficiently large part of the town's population to trigger a referendum on the conduct of the affairs of the municipality in which they live.

Local democracy is destined to become much more direct, because this is where demagogy has the least space: citizens can see the results of disastrous actions much more immediately, and are much more aware of the issues and constraints that weigh on the actions of the town hall.

The new pyramid of powers

Thinking in a different way about how different responsibilities can be combined also helps us to deal with the major transformations of our society. Take the example of the fight against climate change and the protection of biodiversity and the environment.

In line with what we stated in the previous chapter, the role of the European Union in this area is to enable member states to pursue policies that they cannot achieve on their own because they are too expensive for economic producers, because the research efforts are insufficient, or because the market is too small to permit alternative industrial sectors to be set up. In other words, it is up to the European Union to create the general framework for this fight: a price for carbon that will really have an impact on greenhouse gas emissions, with a border tax to avoid unfair competition; a Europe-wide ban on technologies and components that pose a long-term health hazard (for example, endocrine disrupters might one day be viewed in the same way that tobacco and asbestos are today, as often dangerous molecules whose regulation should have diminished the number of diseases and deaths); the funding and coordination of scientific research, for example in the field of energy storage; and the end of our dependence on non-recyclable plastic (particularly in terms of packaging), etc. The fact that the European Union is a mill that grinds very slowly is in this case very useful: it guarantees to all stakeholders – scientists, companies, public administrations – that the policy will not fall victim to those U-turns that sometimes affect national decisions. Of course, if citizens wanted to halt these policies, European elections would make it possible to choose an alternative government that would put an end to them. But, in the event that they support them, it would be desirable to implement them right across the continent, where they would be both more effective and more likely to be consistently applied.

In this framework, states would be encouraged to implement the national policies that ensue. What should be their starting point? The following paradox: there have never been so many citizens willing to fight climate and environmental hazards, and yet green policies rarely seem popular.

One can, of course, wax ironic about the selfishness of these good souls who would not want to give up their personal comforts for the collective good. But we must be less cynical: many citizens are ready to act, but they want to act effectively. However, they do not see the connection between their individual sacrifices and the general cause.

They are first and foremost perplexed by the huge range of available options. Suppose we are ready to make a bit of an extra effort to fight global warming: no one really knows what to do. Would it be better to get a different make of car, to stop eating meat, to use a different kind of light bulb, to stop flying, to eat organic food, or to put electronic equipment on standby? At best, everyone is convinced of the usefulness of these actions but does not know which one to choose, and therefore zigzags between one and the other. At worst, we do nothing. But how many people know that giving up one transatlantic flight a year saves twice as much carbon as stopping eating meat? Or that stopping eating meat is, on average, eight times more effective at combating global warming than using a different kind of light bulb?[1]

There is therefore an urgent need for the public authorities to design, using digital tools, a platform that will allow everyone to know what, in their personal situation, is the most effective and most appropriate action for them to take in this collective struggle. It is easy to imagine everyone being persuaded to provide a few details about their way of life (whether they live in the city or in the countryside, whether or not they travel a lot, their age, etc.) and about the efforts they would be ready to make for the climate and the environment (by giving time and/or money, for example); in return, they would be given suggestions on how to maximize their effects. Where governments have chosen not to wage this campaign (in the United States, and also in Italy, Hungary, Brazil, etc.), it is up to civil society to unite to provide citizens with a raft of choices. The cost will be modest, compared to the results of the actions it will make possible.

But citizens are often perplexed: isn't everything we do futile given the enormity of the task? A second and equally useful step would be for public authorities to inform them of understandable and achievable goals. How can anyone feel concerned by a goal such as 'a 20 per cent reduction in greenhouse gas emissions'? It is so abstract that it is impossible, at first sight, to know how to meet this objective in one's daily life. Do you know, however, that commercial vehicles (those vans that crisscross our streets and roads delivering parcels purchased online and merchandise from our neighbourhood stores) represent a large amount of greenhouse gas emissions (six per cent of total greenhouse gas emissions in France)? This is one example of a concrete and understandable goal: to convert one hundred per cent of the commercial vehicle fleet to electric. This is the responsibility of the public authorities, which can allocate subsidies and draw up more stringent regulations; it is obviously the responsibility of the companies concerned, which must be encouraged to take into consideration the environmental impact of their activity. But it can also become the responsibility of citizens – they can, for example, decide to use companies that have switched to electric vehicles. One could even imagine a mechanism being put in place for individuals to finance a change of vehicles for workers who cannot afford to do so themselves, by resorting to crowdfunding.

This example can be applied to all environmental topics, from reducing fine particle emissions to converting farms to products that are no longer dangerous for bees, not to mention all the little struggles that together comprise the fight against the degradation of our climate and our planet. We must rethink the way the different levels relate to one another, from international action to individual action.

New political movements

For a very long time, political parties have played a key role in enabling poorly educated populations to support and commit to prefabricated doctrines. But citizens today feel quite mature enough to form their own opinions, and look with greater circumspection upon official lines and voting instructions. The traditional political parties have haemorrhaged considerable support. Yet political organizations remain indispensable for a democratic life worthy of the name. In order to give them a fresh impetus, we must start from the relationship they have with their activists.

Traditional political parties see activists as serving the ambitions of their leaders, whom they support within parties and applaud at rallies, and for whom they stick up posters and distribute leaflets. Each activist is at the service of the higher echelons and, ultimately, of a professional whose main purpose is to be elected and then to remain in office at all costs. The root of the chronic difficulties encountered today by the traditional parties is, in our view, very clear: they think only of elections. When they win, it is so that they can better prepare for the next election; when they lose, it is so that they can better prepare their revenge. This is sometimes mere cynicism. Often, it is more simply the consequence of a vision that reduces public action to public policies: without seizing state power or the various local administrative powers, there is no possibility of impacting on reality, getting results, or providing solutions to the concrete problems faced by ordinary citizens. Everything must therefore be used to win or keep these tools; outside campaign periods, partisan apparatuses are increasingly dormant.

At the same time, traditional political parties have lost, one by one, all the attributes which for a long time they alone enjoyed, and on which their monopoly on electoral action rested: the mobilization of supporters, the identification of talents, the machinery for mapping out their territories. When you control Facebook, Twitter or YouTube, you no longer need hundred-year-old political parties to launch a petition, organize an event or engage in local actions.

To survive, these traditional political parties must find a raison d'être, emphasizing the importance of action over elections, groundwork over media impact, citizens and supporters over elected officials. In the absence of such a start, it is a safe bet that over the next few years there will be ever more of the election victories that until recently were judged 'pure fantasy', from that of the unspeakable Donald Trump as President of the United States to that of the comedian Volodymir Zelinsky as President of Ukraine, or the triumph in Brazil of an MP viewed with contempt for twenty years, namely the infamous Jair Bolsonaro.

Now imagine the creation of a progressive political movement of a new kind, of which En Marche! was the first model. It assumes that you pay nothing to join – in many countries this is obvious, but there are still nations in which political parties consider that their activists' money is worth more than their time and commitment. It also accepts that you are free to belong to other parties or political parties: as long as members share the progressivist principles set out by the movement, they are free to be politically active wherever they want (as luck would have it, there are progressivists everywhere).

'Starting at the bottom' means putting each element of the movement's structure at the service of the lower rung. In this movement, the supporter rules. This movement is based on local committees, freely created and administered. Of course, it mobilizes its members in favour of electoral campaigns. But, and this is the key, it mainly mobilizes its members to act without waiting for the next elections, whatever the place, regardless of the number of activists, on whatever issue. Action can target a particular category of people (help with homework, administrative formalities, support for seniors, etc.); it can be done in a localized way (arranging regular meetings to raise awareness about the use of digital resources, for example); it can be done concretely (setting up a shared urban kitchen garden) or in a more dematerialized fashion (creating a group of 'public writers' on the Internet). Politics is not just a matter of elections, and we get as close to progressivist goals by increasing the possibilities of all (first and foremost those with the least) as we do by passing laws. The results are immediate: the commitment of activists is made much more gratifying, because they can see that they are collectively improving the reality around them; the public action of the administration is made much more effective because these different initiatives compensate precisely for the weakness in traditional public policies, at the most local and most individualized level of their application, by going that last little extra mile towards reform; finally, the citizens who are the witnesses and sometimes the beneficiaries of these actions change the way they view politics.

Note that this is different from the mode of 'participatory democracy', which consists of seeing its members as a purely electoral body that is consulted regularly to endorse the decisions of the management on the programme to be defended or the candidates to be selected at elections. Instead, the point is to transform every progressivist into a real creator of progress – a 'progressor'.

Of course, the political movement we are talking about would have the potential to present candidates for elections at all levels, so as to effect on a grand scale what the multitude of local progressivist groups have effected on the small scale. These candidates would not be envisaging a professional political career: their election would be a stage in their commitment.

This is the model on which we based En Marche!, the French movement that, in 2017, ended almost sixty years of political monopoly on the part of the two traditional parties of 'left' and 'right' by winning in rapid succession the presidential election and the parliamentary elections. But there is still much to be done, including in France, to sustain this model. Its first two years, devoted entirely to the government of the country, have not been the most conducive to cultivating this dimension: this is one of the great challenges facing us.

From fake politics to fake news

We wish to conclude this chapter by emphasizing a point which must be the beginning of any progressivist action and the precondition for any election: the establishment of a diagnosis. It seems to us that the impotence into which politics has fallen over the past forty years stems from the fact that it could no longer see society as it really is.

For aspiring candidates, spending time listening to problems seems a huge waste of time. They feel that the difficulties are obvious: unemployment, delinquency, and so on. They think in all sincerity that citizens expect answers from them – quick and simple answers: what policies are they proposing for the economy or for security issues? Candidates want to go directly from symptoms to treatment.

On the contrary, we believe that the diagnosis stage is crucial. It is typically deployed in three stages. First, people must listen to the requests of their fellow citizens: they are often more informed and more nuanced than the polls or snatched conversations might suggest. Next, they must rely on the wealth of knowledge available to gauge the depth of the problem and its implications: this consultation must be broad and public. Executive power is often ill at ease doing this. MPs can play a crucial role here, investigating, collecting information, assessing the public action taken – in short, laying bare whatever is ignored or unspoken. Finally, this work must be made public, and the difficulties encountered as well as the avenues available should be shared with everyone. We are all capable of understanding the often difficult choices we face if only we have the reason explained to us. Exposing these dilemmas would not tarnish the prestige of politicians, as some may fear. Quite the contrary, it would refurbish it. By clarifying the process of decision-making, we provide for a credible alternative to simplistic assumptions and suspicions.

What is the point?

First, it is important to make sure that representatives tackle the right issues. We can accept that politicians find it difficult to respond quickly to our problems: they are not all easy, or even possible, to solve. But it is intolerable when politicians respond to *other* problems because they have not looked closely enough at our lives. In France, La Grande Marche[2] – both the first action launched by En Marche! and the largest door-to-door operation ever launched in the country outside of an election campaign – demonstrated that one of the main bugbears of the French was quite simply 'politics' (that is, the way politics worked), even though this item was not included in any of the traditional barometers used by polling organizations.

It is also essential to ensure that citizens have a clear perception of social reality. This is not always the case. This is true even when it comes to their own position in society. We invite you to carry out a little exercise that reflects the difficulty of this task, and the gap that often exists between perception and reality, even in the eyes of knowledgeable citizens: at your next family meal, or your next dinner party with friends, ask everyone where they think they stand on the income ladder. Then ask them to check, by using this online tool which, when you enter your net monthly income, tells you how you compare with other citizens in your country: http://www.compareyourincome.org. Everyone can do this quite discreetly, but they must all say at the end whether their initial perception of their own situation was right or not. We promise you will be surprised!

These examples should not lead us to underestimate the great difficulty of establishing a firm diagnosis, one that can be shared by the greatest number of people. This presupposes that, first and foremost, we face up directly to the things that are hurting. For example, we bet that not many French people are aware that our free educational system is one of the most inegalitarian in any of the developed countries – in the very country of equality! But this is just as true in the United States, where the image of the self-made man has retained such power that it still stops too many from realizing that inequalities there have returned to the same level as at the beginning of the twentieth century, and that life expectancy has been falling since 2014. And who knows that the state of the German infrastructure is hardly better than in the countries of the former USSR – or that nearly half the bridges in Germany need rebuilding?[3]

That's why we believe that a correct diagnosis will help to tackle the real problems in the best possible way once elections are won. And whoever has made the correct diagnosis of reality and communicated it to others will have gained the right to be heard and followed by his or her fellow-citizens.

Today, for lack of a common vision of society and its challenges, a vision that will reflect what everyone can see in their lives, we have allowed alternative, crazy visions to flourish, in the form of fake news. People often wonder about the *supply* of fake news, about the way the Internet has allowed rumours to spread with unprecedented speed and made it possible for foreign powers to manipulate such rumours. These questions are perfectly necessary. But we must also wonder about the *demand* – what makes fake news credible in the eyes of what, after all, are the most educated populations in the history of humanity? The answer is that the official discourse seems equally improbable to them:[4] because it does not respond to their worries or their anxieties, the news on TV seems to describe a world every bit as unreal as the ever-spiralling trail of emails into which their friends and relatives drag them.

That's why governments seem just as untrustworthy to them as the first rumour they come across: citizens believe in 'fake news' because what they can also observe is 'fake politics'.

The fake news of the so-called Marrakesh Pact claimed, for example, against all common sense, that governments were about to sign a treaty authorizing uncontrolled immigration into Western countries. We know that this was exploited by the American far right, and spread like wildfire through Internet forums and social networks, leading to the overthrow of the Belgian government. But the fact that it generated so many passions reveals something more profound – that the political treatment of immigration is quite inadequate, since citizens are willing to believe that their leaders are not defending their borders, but striving to destroy them.

5

Populist suicide

We must learn to live together as brothers or perish together as fools.

Martin Luther King, 'Remaining Awake Through a Great Revolution', speech of 31 March 1968

We saw in Chapter 1 how the ideal of autonomy has been imposed since the eighteenth century as the only one worth pursuing. After two centuries of struggle, access to a wide range of individual rights and an economic model tempering the dynamic of the market with a (more or less) high degree of redistribution is now the rule in all developed countries. This is the legacy of the interplay between the parties of the left and the right. It is a precious legacy for everyone, but it is problematic for them. Precious, because it is much less disputed, especially in Western Europe. Problematic, because it means the end of left and right: they have exhausted what lay at the heart of their contrast and their complementarity, and have not had the daring to reinvent themselves in face of the new challenges.

From frustration to revolt

There are, however, many things that need to be done if freedom is to be translated from idea into actuality, as we also showed in Chapter 1. Indeed, it is probably an endless fight. The gap between speech and reality has created a growing frustration, pent-up in silence for a long time, scarcely perceptible and still less expressed – but now it has finally become open revolt.

Those who have been left stranded by history, the excluded and the despised, gradually understood that something was wrong with society. They were filled with rage against the old parties, not only because the latter were partly responsible for their predicament, but mostly because they refused even to recognize it. Those traditional parties acted like a doctor who, flying in the face of all the evidence, tells a patient writhing in pain: 'It's all in your head; I can assure you there's nothing wrong with you!'

There were more and more electoral warnings. The old parties ignored them. After denial came the time of cynicism. They thought they could confine the revolt to a few sections of the population, or even use it to consolidate the ranks of their own voters. In the United Kingdom, the creation of UKIP, for long a tiny group advocating Britain's exit from the European Union, allowed Labour and Conservatives to indulge in endless tactical manoeuvres in countless elections. In the United States, the cartoon caricature Donald Trump was initially perceived as a blessing by the Democrats who were delighted to see him upset the Republican primaries. In France, dramatizing the fight against the National Front long allowed the Socialist Party to reap a double dividend: it could mobilize its troops at a time when it no longer had a more positive programme to propose, and it could divide the right at a time when the latter was not ready to consider an alliance with a Front National still tarnished by memories of the Second World War.

This was a drastic mistake. The National Front got through to the final stage of the last French presidential election. Donald Trump seized the White House. The British have decided to leave Europe.

Revolt is logically rooted among those for whom the gap between the ideal of autonomy and the reality was the greatest, and in whom frustration was therefore the most acute. The others have, for a longer time, showed restraint or blindness, sometimes out of habit, often also because they are satisfied with their privileged access to resources such as education or innovation.

But then the conflagration spread to every level of society. Twenty years ago, attention was drawn to the 'excluded' (the unemployed, the least well-off, the residents of neighbourhoods where poverty and immigration were concentrated). Ten years ago, the secession of the working classes (often workers from the regions devastated by deindustrialization) was finally noticed, and there was talk of the 'losers of globalization', from the American rust belt to the Marche region of Italy. Now the heart of society, the middle classes themselves, are questioning the established order. We expect that, very soon, fringes of the higher echelons will in turn resort to revolt.

No barracks, kolkhoz or convent

A renewed political movement then arose, in the shape of what is known as 'populism'. It is not strictly speaking an ideology, because most of the time it has neither the characteristics nor any pretence to be one. It is not a programme either, because it differs according to the country (for example, Donald Trump and Jair Bolsonaro are economically liberal, while Marine Le Pen favours strong regulation of the economy), changes over time (Marine Le Pen has repeatedly changed her opinion on the need to leave the European Union, Viktor Orbán's policy alternates between flexibilization and state control) and can form very surprising alliances (such as that between the Five Star Movement and the Northern League in Italy). It is essentially a strategy based on a particular intuition.

The intuition is summed up by the phrase 'take back control', the famous slogan of the Brexiters, with its variants in the several countries where populists are on the move. It is a powerful way of gathering support as it lies at the intersection between a legitimate collective demand (after all, what is democracy if not the power of the people?) and an individual suffering that has been ignored. As we have explained, dispossession in the face of major changes such as globalization, multiculturalism and individualization, changes praised wholeheartedly and with great naivety by many liberals, had helped to give birth to an immense sense of frustration in Western societies.

The strategy, on the other hand, does not aim at solving the real questions posed by these transformations. It consists in arrogating to itself the monopoly of the representation of the 'people', in attributing exclusively the misfortunes that are overwhelming it to a specific enemy outside the community (mainly elites, but also immigrants, sometimes the 'rich', etc.), in exploiting anger, fanning it if necessary with fake news and disinformation, and undermining independent institutions one by one (the media, central banks, the judiciary, and so on).[1]

How are populists situated in relation to 'progress', as embodied for example in the conquest of autonomy? Is it simply a question of proposing a different and doubtless dangerous path to the same goal? Populists have a great deal to say about the so-called evils of current society, but very little about the society they defend. Nevertheless, the implicit conclusion of their stance lies poles apart from any 'progress': for populists, there is nothing left to create, to discover or to think, and hardly any new possibilities, just clashes. All they propose is to confiscate or exclude; so they give up on progress and the future. This is why populist parties are all parties of capitulation. One need merely look more closely at their favourite themes to realize this.

The populism of the far right (that of Donald Trump, Matteo Salvini, Viktor Orbán, Jair Bolsonaro and all those who dream of imitating them) proposes freezing our identities. Everything is foreordained in our traditions, if not in our genes. Nations have no future but only a past. The ulterior motives at work here are all too clear: it is easy to turn the foreign peril into a bogeyman and see it as the sole cause of all our ills. This resonates with the anxieties – sometimes understandable – caused by immigration or globalization, and it also provides a scape-goat that will stir the masses while concealing the narrowness and weakness of the proposed solutions.

But let's pause here for a moment, and examine what some of their language says when taken literally. Those who speak this language claim they are defending our 'identity'. Does a pro-gressivist believe by definition that identity doesn't exist? Of course not. But what are we talking about when we talk about identity? Take the example of France. Identity isn't rooted in a particular era – for what was the most 'French' society: that of General de Gaulle, Napoleon, Robespierre or Clovis? It isn't an ideology to be promoted: is a person more French by being Republican with Georges Clemenceau or monarchist with Georges Bernanos; European with Victor Hugo or nationalist with Charles Péguy; liberal with Alexis de Tocqueville or rev-olutionary with Jean-Paul Sartre? It's not a cuisine, an artistic style, a fashion: there have been so many of these in our past. France is a succession of layers, of successive contributions, which have mingled together, allowed the culture to grow and spread without ever getting lost. The same argument applies to every country in the world. Our identity is one thing and one thing alone: a memory. No one can be excluded from memory; no one can be the sole repository of memory. French people whose families have been living in France for countless genera-tions can lose it, and recent immigrants can acquire it.

Is there a 'threat to identity'? Yes. Progressivists would be wrong to deny it: we are indeed seeing the threads that connect us to this past unravelling one by one. But the battle for our identity is not primarily a question of borders, but a question of culture. It is not primarily a matter of local regulations, but of education. When children no longer know the great dates of our history, make grammatical mistakes, or do not acquire enough vocabulary, they endanger this age-old edifice much more than when they refuse to eat pork.

To lose that memory is to condemn yourself to failure. But to do nothing with this memory is to condemn yourself just as surely to impotence. Identity populism, if taken to its logical conclusion, in all its various incarnations, seems to have no other aim than the preservation of the existing order – without even being able to say, as we have seen, what exactly should be preserved of it, divided as it is between sometimes contradictory values and traditions. For the populists, new generations have nothing to invent and nothing to express; all they can do is mourn the loss of what once was. It's is a very depressing programme, at least for those who are not yet dead – in fact, it's a dead end.

Like all political dead ends, it forces its supporters to resort to illusions, fits of madness and wilful distortions to prevent the voters, for as long as possible, from realizing that the promised goal is a mirage. Enemies and conspiracies are invented to explain why arrival in the Promised Land is going to be delayed.

Like all dead ends, populism leads inexorably to a blank wall. The populism of the far left proposes freezing our economies. The economy can no longer create: it merely has to redistribute. By turning the 'elites', the 'oligarchies' or the 'rich' into scapegoats, the supporters of this form of populism actually condemn any form of success and initiative: there's no need to create what we lack – we can just take it from those who already have it. There's no place in the economy for entrepreneurship, and no place in education for excellence. Some people may have felt that this view had been finally disproved by the failure of all communist regimes, which never led to free and prosperous societies – after all, the day when individual initiative is stifled, everyone loses. But these people were wrong: politics is different from science in that we can repeat the same mistakes over and over again. The response to economic failure can only be a change in policy, or else repression. Already, these parties leave little room for initiatives beyond the leader's control. The revolutionary slogans of the radical left, however, are now again finding an audience among all those who have gradually been excluded from the system.

Progressivists may, of course, share the anger of these movements, the anger that was expressed at the the Puerta del Sol or by the rebels of Occupy Wall Street, or by the supporters of the 'Nuit debout'.[2] But they know what happens when their protest is commandeered by the far left. The violence of the methods and the language of the far left add to the misfortunes of the world – misfortunes it is claiming to fight. A handful of leftist individuals claim to know *for* the people, *on behalf of* the people, what is good for them. La France insoumise in France, Podemos in Spain, Corbynism in the United Kingdom are all on the same slippery slope. Far-left populism is not interested in people, but in the masses. It is not interested in the people, but in the crowd.

These initiatives have always produced undesirable results: a negation of the diversity and richness of the possibilities of each individual; blind faith in the Party and its leader and manipulation of the people; social and political misery, and the reduction of individual and public liberties. If they were in power and wanted to stay there, far left populists would inevitably have to choose between violence and a U-turn: Mélenchon and Corbyn and their ilk always end up either as Maduro or as Tsipras.

As well as these populisms, a third form of capitulation threatens: fundamentalism. Without even referring to its most violent and criminal manifestations, it is highly important for progressivists not to underestimate the danger of this creed, for fear of encouraging, for instance, far-right manipulations.

Fundamentalists propose that we abdicate our free will. Everything, they say, is written in the sacred books. There is nothing for human beings to discuss on Earth: they need only listen to Heaven. All dimensions of our existence should be subject to the most literal and rigorous interpretations of religious dogmas. Fundamentalists too have their scapegoats: unbelievers, 'infidels', apostates. Nothing is more common to fundamentalists than the more or less overt, more or less violent, persecution of women and LGBT+ people. Admittedly, this threat is of a different nature from the two previous ones. It does not have the same history and does not take the same forms. But it too is a response to the frustrations that the betrayal of the promise of autonomy has left in its wake. Essentially, it is the most radical opponent of progress and tries to transform our lives without relying on elections. If implemented, it would negate our first principle: the emancipated exploration of possibilities has no meaning for those whose individual duty lies in respecting the letter of religious edicts. Some elements of the battle for same-sex marriage were part of this fight, as was the daily struggle, in suburbs and rough neighbourhoods, for women to be treated as absolute equals to men. But fundamentalism also attacks our second principle: it drags its flock into a gradual secession from the nation as a whole. Acting together then becomes impossible. Islam is particularly prone to a radical streak that provides an outlet for people of immigrant origin but also – as evidenced by the number of conversions – for individuals who do not belong to families of Muslim tradition. Other religions are sliding or are likely to slide into the same tendency. It would be a big mistake for progressivists to take this threat lightly, and to believe that they are absolved from fighting against it on the pretext that it can shelter behind religious liberty. They must fight it, politically and culturally, as they would any dangerous ideology.

Depending on the country and the party, these three forms can of course hybridize. You can have the barracks, the kolkhoz, or the convent. The strength of the populists lies in their ability to persuade others that they have heard the sufferings of the people. This is often a staged claim – after all, many populist leaders come as much from the political elite as do their opponents – but it is generally put forward with some skill. It works, because it paints a disastrous picture of the alternatives.

The weakness of the populists lies in their programme. This is because all their programmes are forms of surrender. They do not believe in the expansion of collective and individual possibilities. Helping human beings to gain autonomy is of no interest to them. More than their violence or their provocations, more than their incompetence or their dishonesty, this is their real Achilles heel: unlike the doctor we talked about earlier, they have heard the pain of their patients, but they don't waste a second on trying to heal them. 'Does it hurt when I press? Yes? What about when I press harder?' They devote all their energy not to treating their patients, but to convincing them that they can hear their cries.

This is less intolerable than denial, but it's still painful, and just as ineffective. Let's look at the countries where populists have taken power. If they were truly able to respond to the aspirations of the people, we should see their passions subside and life resume its ordinary course. It's quite the opposite. Elections are usually just a headlong flight forward. The fate of the populists can already be foretold.

Populism stems from a democratic aspiration: that of having one's suffering and frustration finally heard and taken into account by the rulers; that of seeing politics regaining control. In the second and third chapters, we saw how fully legitimate this aspiration was.

They also thrive on misunderstandings. They claim that it would be enough to have a 'good leader' at the helm, one who could inspire people to act. But we saw in the third and fourth chapters that the whole of society needs to be reformed if we really want to find room for manoeuvre. Collective autonomy implies more autonomy for all citizens rather than more arbitrary power for their leader. Populists believe that it would be enough to neutralize a few scapegoats in order for us to regain control of our lives, but facts are stubborn and it takes only a short while for the population to realize that immigration is not the cause of all its problems, and that it is not enough to leave the European Union, or to rob the rich, for everyday life to get better.

The populists then slide into authoritarian mode: they designate new scapegoats to justify their own inability to transform people's lives. They steadily attack all the countervailing powers that stand in their way (an independent judiciary, a free press, central banks), in one last attempt to hide their fear of having to be accountable to them too. This crazed attempt to outbid all others will inevitably come to an end. But at what cost? That of the suicide of our societies.

This is why we need to foreground as quickly as possible the alternative to this first category of responses to the society of frustration.

Building up a majority

This alternative cannot come from traditional parties, left or right, Conservative or Labour, Republican or Democrat, at least not in their present form and with their current staff, because they have lost all credibility in the eyes of voters. If these parties are to get out of their rut, they need to radically question themselves – and to begin with, they need to sack all those who got them stuck in the rut.

Populists of both the far left and the far right follow different paths but use the same strategy to come to power – they exploit the sense of rebellion, they claim to represent the 'people' alone, and they point the finger at scapegoats. Indeed, this is essentially how we recognize them. In a way, everything else is interchangeable because it is incidental. That's why we believe that a more or less underground movement of populist convergence is already at work. This has happened in Italy, for example, with the coalition between the Five Star Movement and the Northern League; in the United Kingdom, in the way Jeremy Corbyn's Labour Party has equivocated over the question of Brexit; and in France, where Jean-Luc Mélenchon refused to choose between the far right of Marine Le Pen and the progressivism of Emmanuel Macron in the second round of the last presidential election. We therefore believe that a convergence must also take place on the side of the progressivists – all those who feel that a real autonomy can be created for each and every person – whatever their possible political origin, if they even have one.

On which forces can such a convergence rely, at a time when rebels are increasingly drifting into the populist camp? And above all, how can they be identified? Electoral strategy is usually a secret, one considered to be too shameful to be disclosed to voters, or too sensitive to be shared with activists. It is therefore the preserve of candidates and their close entourage. We wish, instead, to bring it out into the open. This is all the more necessary as the classical method is out of date.

Traditional electorates ('socialists', 'centrists' and so on) are shrinking. The main political 'group', in the electoral sense of the term, is usually made up of non-voters. We cannot therefore rest content with targeting the voters for this or that particular man or woman, or the heirs of a particular political current. We must start all over again.

More generally, the politics of the electoral bloc, which simply combined social categories to form a majority, can no longer apply. Electoral behaviour has never been so independent of traditional social categories, and never so dependent on how individuals view their own lives and futures. That is why workers no longer vote as a unified category – no more than 'Latinos', 'Muslims', 'the younger generation', cadres, farmers, etc. This is exactly what we saw in the last French presidential election, with very unusual motives for voting behaviour. One of the main common points of Emmanuel Macron's voters was the fact that they overwhelmingly declared themselves to be 'optimistic'[3] Conversely, recent research has shown that a key determinant of the vote for Marine Le Pen, and more generally for right-wing populism, was a very low level of 'interpersonal trust', something that has to do with much more subtle factors than simply income, employment or education, and which relates for instance to one's personal history, family and local traditions, and so on.[4]

The deadly error – exactly the one that Emmanuel Macron's victorious campaign avoided – would then be to identify a few fractions of the supposedly natural electorate (executives, residents of big cities, ethnic or religious minorities), compile a catalogue of their demands, promise to satisfy them, hope that the combination of these fractions will ensure a majority in the ballot box ... and turn a blind eye to the rest of the population.

To act like that is an act of betrayal, a mistake and a misapprehension. First, it is a betrayal: progressivists would become neither more useful nor more sincere than their opponents if they stopped trying to open up new possibilities for all, including – and especially – for those who did not vote for them. Second, it is a strategic mistake: it leads inexorably, once power has been won, to serving only a narrow clientele, as have all traditional parties for so long, leading an increasing number of sectors of society to slide into revolt. Finally, it is a misapprehension about its potential voters: the best way to protect their possibilities is to enable the whole of society to benefit from them. This is a crucial point, because it is not uncommon for progressive voters to have difficulty understanding it. They may wonder why they should grant additional public funds to a particular city or region which is a populist bastion rather than to the place they themselves live in. Why increase the numbers of teachers in classes in which their own children will never set foot? Why recruit new police officers to patrol neighbourhoods where they don't live? Simply because, by patiently making the populations who live in these places stakeholders in the promise of autonomy, we will deprive populists of their support.

This strategy is the riskiest: it necessarily leads to defending proposals that are not always popular. It's the only strategy that sees every voter as a citizen to persuade, and not as an idiot to be fooled. It's the only strategy that, in case of victory, provides a clear mandate to act. In short, it's the only strategy possible for those who want to change reality rather than instrumental-izing it or setting it in stone.

Our electoral strategy can therefore be summed up in one sentence: progressivists must not create the policies of their majority but a majority from their policies.[5]

So there will be no more any identifiable front lines. Unlike in the old days, when right and left knew they could appeal only to well-defined socio-professional categories (workers in one case, craftsmen and craftswomen in the other), both progressivists and populists can now appeal to people within any social category. It is no coincidence that social networks already play such an important role in election campaigns: they allow messages to be personalized to an unprecedented level. The political struggle ahead will not be, as many think, a trench war, class against class, but a war of movement, across society and involving every individual.

The progressivists have the following plan: they need to convince the optimists to conquer power (this is what happened in France in 2017); they should exercise this power to open up 'possibilities' for the pessimists (this is what is happening in France); and finally, they should demonstrate to pessimists that their potential situation has really changed. Then the progres-sivists will have won.

Conclusion

This is the social situation today: on the one hand, an unprecedented triumph of the aspiration to autonomy across social circles and across borders. On the other hand, a growing sense of frustration with all the obstacles this aspiration encounters. Yesterday, traditional parties seemed eternal. Today, for lack of positive projects, it is they who are condemned to be eroded by forces that had been thought consigned to the dustbin of history. The result is that nobody cares about progress any more. Nobody looks at social reality to see how greatly it differs from traditional representations. No one trusts individuals, either as decision makers for themselves or as actors of collective change.

It is this torch that the new progressivists must take back. We have shown that they have formidable opponents: populist parties that capitalize on citizens' despair and try to make capitulation desirable by freezing their economy or their identity; and religious fundamentalism, which proposes to make them abdicate their free will. We have shown that progressivism has a future (better: that progressivism *is* the future), on the condition that it aims at the maximization of the possibilities of individuals (present and future), recognizes that there are more possibilities when we act together, and seeks to start from the bottom: these are the three principles of the new progressivism that we have tried to define in these pages.

Elections have confirmed, country by country, that the old split between right and left has long since run out of steam. But while a new confrontation between progressivists and populists may very often correspond to the current or emerging situation, it is not a very pleasant prospect. It is a particularly unstable and dangerous situation. When the populists are in opposition, no glass ceiling stops them from coming to power: complacently persisting in their demonization, hoping that they will be strong enough to quell rivals but not strong enough ever to form a majority, is a very risky ploy for their opponents. This is a lesson that the American Democrats cruelly learned in 2016 and that we must always remember. When the populists are in power, we are also forced to realize that we are far from the 'normalization' that some hoped to see emerge from contact with the realities of government: it is, on the contrary, a headlong flight forwards and a radicalization of policies that often ensue. We do not have the right to expect them to come to a halt quickly and spontaneously.

Progressivists must not be satisfied by a clash with the populists. On the contrary: they must lay the basis for a new age in our political life by establishing a clinical diagnosis of the failures of the traditional parties and by methodically responding to the frustration expressed in the populist vote. Then, and only then, this vote may start to shrink.

The heart of the political fight is not the fight against the other parties, it is a confrontation with reality. This must go well beyond the usual circle of professionals in the electoral game. It should not be enough to bring citizens into politics, especially in the run-up to elections; rather, politics should be brought to the citizens. This process starts today, at the most local and concrete level, as we saw in the fourth chapter. You may be convinced by the content of this book, but still not wish to commit yourself politically. Don't close our book with a feeling of resentment: it's not 'politically' that counts, but 'to commit'. For this, there is no need to favour one fight over another, nor to relegate community or cultural actions to a secondary place.

Our final message is very simple. If you are generally in agreement with what you have read, know that you are not alone – we can even bet that, all together, we are more numerous than those who have chosen rent (the traditional parties) or capitulation (the populist parties). But know also that it is time to commit. There is nothing inevitable about the movement for which we are calling. It needs to start again from the bottom – in its thinking, in its organization, in its action.

Progress will never again fall from the sky. It's a story on a human scale. The story of a grassroots progressivism.[1]

Notes

1 The society of frustration

1 We rely here on the French philosopher and historian Marcel Gauchet's narrative, especially *L'Avènement de la Démocratie IV*, *Le nouveau monde* (Paris: Gallimard, 2017).

2 We rely here on Marcel Gauchet, *La gauche au défi de la société des individus* (Paris: Fondation européenne d'études progressistes et Fondation Jean Jaurès, 2016).

3 Gauchet, *La gauche au défi de la société des individus*.

4 See Marcel Gauchet, 'Right and Left', in Pierre Nora (ed.), *Realms of Memory. The Construction of the French Past*, 4 vols. (1999–2010), vol. 1, *Conflicts and Divisions*, trans. Arthur Goldhammer (Chicago, IL: Chicago University Press, 1999), pp. 241–300.

5 For the situation in the United States, see Tyler Cowen, *The Complacent Class: The Self-Defeating Quest for the American Dream* (New York: St Martin's Press, 2017).

6 'Les femmes ont gagné en moyenne 16 pour cent de moins que les hommes dans l'UE en 2016', Eurostat, 7 March 2018.

7 Marianne Bertrand and Sendhil Mullainathan, 'Are Emily and Greg More Employable than Lakisha and Jamal? A Field

Experiment on Labor Market Discrimination', *American Economic Review*, 2005

8 Marie-Anne Valfort, 'Discriminations à l'embauche: une réalité' (Institut Montaigne, October 2015).

9 Daniel Cohen, *The Infinite Desire for Growth* (Princeton, NJ: Princeton University Press, 2018).

10 'A Broken Social Elevator? How to Promote Social Mobility' (OECD, June 2018).

11 Cohen, *The Infinite Desire for Growth*.

12 Cohen, *The Infinite Desire for Growth*.

13 Éric Maurin, *Le Ghetto français* (Paris: Le Seuil, 2006), p. 13.

14 Pierre Courtioux and Vincent Lignon, 'Avoir un diplôme pour faire une bonne carrière ou un bon mariage?' (EDHEC Business School, 2014).

15 https://streeteasy.com/blog/nyc-housing-market-financial-crisis-one-decade-later/.

16 Jochen Möbert, 'The German Housing Market in 2018' (Deutsche Bank Research, 2018) https://www.dbresearch.com/PROD/RPS_EN-PROD/PROD0000000000460528/The_German_housing_market_in_2018.pdf.

17 https://www.home.co.uk/guides/house_prices_report.htm?location=london&all=1.

18 Thomas Piketty, *Capital in the Twenty-First Century*, trans. Arthur Goldhammer (Cambridge, MA and London: The Belknap Press, Harvard University Press, 2014), p. 284.

19 Piketty, *Capital*, p. 175.

20 Cowen, *The Complacent Class*.

21 Joseph Stiglitz, *Rewriting the Rules of the American Economy:*

An Agenda for Growth and Shared Prosperity (New York: W.W. Norton and Company, 2015), p. 59.

2 Maximizing possibilities (or the first principle of progressivism)

1 Judith Scott-Clayton, 'The looming student loan default crisis is worse than we thought', Brookings Institution, 11 January 2018. https://www.brookings.edu/research/the-looming-student-loan-default-crisis-is-worse-than-we-thought/.

2 Son Thierry Ly (rapporteur), 'Quelle finalité pour quelle école ?' (France Stratégie, 2016, p. 12).

3 Joseph Stiglitz, *Rewriting the Rules of the American Economy: An Agenda for Growth and Shared Prosperity* (New York: W.W. Norton and Company, 2015), p. 13.

4 Thomas Philippon, 'Has the US Finance Industry Become Less Efficient?', *American Economic Review*, 2015.

5 Guillaume Bazot, 'Financial Consumption and Cost of Finance, Measuring Financial Efficiency in Europe (1950–2007)', *Journal of the European Economic Association*, 16, 2018.

6 We rely again on the the work of Thomas Philippon; in particular 'The FinTech Opportunity' (*NBER Working Paper*, 2016).

7 This argument is convincingly made by Luigi Zingales. See the interview 'Are Google and Facebook Monopolies?', *Chicago Booth Review*, 22 January 2018.

8 Joseph Stiglitz, *Rewriting the Rules of the American Economy*.

9 Paul-Adrien Hyppolite and Antoine Michon discuss several of these suggestions: see their *Les géants du numérique (2): un frein à*

l'innovation? (Fondation pour l'innovation politique, November 2018).

10 This idea is defended by Luigi Zingales and Guy Rolnik in 'A Way to Own Your Social Data', *The New York Times*, 30 June 2017.

3 There are more possibilities when we act together (or the second principle of progressivism)

1 Marcel Gauchet, *La démocratie contre elle-même* (Paris: Gallimard, 2002).

2 Xavier Ragot, *Civiliser le capitalisme* (Paris: Fayard, 2019).

3 This is a swathe of low-density population running across France from the north-east to the south-west. (Translator's note.)

4 See Baptiste Perrissin Fabert and Marion Cauvet, *Les monnaies locales: vers un développement responsable – la transition écologique et solidaire des territoires* (Paris: Editions de la rue d'Ulm, 2018) for an interesting overview of these initiatives and the means to support them.

5 Thomas R. Tørsløv, Ludvig S. Vier and Gabriel Zucman, 'The Missing Profits of Nations', *NBER Working Paper* no. 24701, 2018.

6 For a provocative history of the European Union in this light, see Andrew Moravcsik, *The Choice for Europe: Social Purpose and the State Power from Messina to Maastricht* (Ithaca, NY: Cornell University Press, 1998).

7 More detailed suggestions have been made by Maria Demertzis et al., 'One Size Does Not Fit All'; see 'https://bruegel.

org/2018/09/one-size-does-not-fit-all/.

8 For a vivid analysis of how recent crises shaped the EU, see Luuk van Middelaar, *Alarums and Excursions: Improvising Politics on the European Stage* (Agenda Publishing, 2019).

9 See the work by American psychologist Jonathan Haidt, *The Righteous Mind, Why Good People Are Divided by Politics and Religion* (London: Penguin Books, 2012).

10 For a detailed analysis of these collective feelings, see Haidt, *The Righteous Mind*.

11 For a sharp critique of this liberal ethics, see Hartmut Rosa, *Resonance. A Sociology of Our Relationship to the World*, trans. James C. Wagner (Cambridge: Polity, 2019).

4 Starting from the bottom (or the third principle of progressivism)

1 Seth Wynes and Kimberly A. Nicolas, 'The Climate Mitigation Gap: Education and Government Recommendations Miss the most Effective Individual Actions', *Environmental Research Letters*, 12 July 2017.

2 This 'great march' was not so much a march as a mass operation to gauge public opinion by going round knocking on people's doors. (Translator's note.)

3 Lise Joly, 'Allemagne: transports en commun vétustes, ponts impraticables ... les infrastructures publiques à bout de souffle', France Info, 23 September 2017.

4 This is the hypothesis formulated by Marcel Gauchet in 'La guerre des vérités', *Le Débat*, no. 197, November–December 2017.

5 Populist suicide

1 See Jan-Werner Müller, *What is Populism?* (Philadelphia, PA: University of Pennsylvania Press, 2016).

2 This was a protest against labour reforms; it spread through France in the spring of 2016.

3 Seventy per cent of those who voted for Emmanuel Macron in the first round of the presidential election said they were optimistic about the future, as against 45 per cent of all those polled and 29 per cent of those who voted for Marine Le Pen ('L'état d'esprit des Français: vague 37', IFOP opinion poll for *Dimanche Ouest France*, August 2017).

4 Yann Algan, Elizabeth Beasley, Daniel Cohen and Martial Foucault, *Les origines du populisme: Enquête sur un schisme politique et social* (Paris: Le Seuil, 2019).

5 This debate cuts across all political groups – witness the words of the political scientist Laurent Bouvet who, addressing the French Socialist Party, suggested that instead of 'building the necessarily limited project of a diminished sociology', they build 'the sociology that would favour a great political project' (*Le Sens du peuple* [Paris: Gallimard, 2011], p. 285). On the other hand, Olivier Ferrand, Romain Prudent and Bruno Jeanbart, in a report for Terra Nova ('Gauche: quelle majorité électorale pour 2012?', 10 May 2011), suggested that the left rely on 'its new natural electorate: the France of tomorrow'.

Conclusion

1 David Amiel and Ismaël Emelien, 'A Grassroots Antidote to Populism', Project Syndicate, 25 June 2019.